The Anatomy of Supervision

The Anatomy of Supervision

Developing Learning and Professional Competence for Social Work Students

Derek Gardiner

The Society for Research into Higher Education
& Open University Press

Published by SRHE and
Open University Press
12 Cofferidge Close
Stony Stratford
Milton Keynes MK11 1BY

and
242 Cherry Street
Philadelphia, PA 19106, USA

First Published 1989

British Library Cataloguing in Publication Data

Gardiner, Derek
  The anatomy of supervision: teaching and
  learning for professional competence
  1. Welfare work. Supervision
  I. Title
  361.3′068

  ISBN 0-335-09573-9
  ISBN 0-335-09572-0 (pbk)

Library of Congress Catalog Number Available

Typeset by Rowland Phototypesetting Limited
Bury St Edmunds, Suffolk
Printed in Great Britain by St Edmundsbury Press Limited
Bury St Edmunds, Suffolk

For Fiona and my parents

Contents

Preface

This book is a substantially revised version of a doctoral thesis which reported research into teaching and learning in placement supervision in social work courses. The research was registered at the Institute of Education in the University of London, because it seemed that developments in research methodology and adult learning theory were better established in higher education generally than in social work education.

That decision allowed the development of different perspectives and approaches to studying the content and processes of education, which might have been difficult (or even impossible) within a University Social Work Department. These perspectives involve a shift, from trying to *quantify* how successfully students learn from an educational activity, to *qualitative* accounts of their subjective experience of teaching and learning. This kind of approach allows the possibility of exploring how teaching and learning takes place, and its relationship to the outcomes of that learning.

As adults mature, so they recognize that their world is complex rather than simple; and that in order to comprehend or make sense of their diverse experiences, they must interpret them in the light of increasingly complex constructions of the world. This focus, on how people construe their world, and make it meaningful, is at the heart of recent educational research which relates how the conceptions people have of their world have an impact on their behaviour and on the meanings they attach to their experience. The conceptions people hold of *learning* vary considerably, and may promote or constrain their behaviour in educational activities.

In some ways, this book describes a journey through social work education: first as a student, later supervising students as Head of a Student Unit, and in recent years working for the validating body. This journey covers a substantial period of change in the personal social services from the specialist departments and training courses of the pre-Seebohm days (I trained as a Psychiatric Social Worker), through the expansion of the generic agencies and courses in the 1970s, to the retrenchment and harsher climate for the public sector in the 1980s.

Throughout that period, debates about how to improve social work courses have identified the practice component as crucial, but most in need of improvement. Those discussions and policy developments have been be-devilled by the lack of good evaluative research evidence to provide the basis for judging *quality* in learning, teaching, and assessment. This book is a contribution to those debates; my own view is that whilst there is much to be improved in the practice component of qualifying courses, there are equally urgent problems to be addressed in the educational institutions.

This lack of evidence poses particular problems for researchers, because there is no tradition of research into social work education to rely upon for the design and implementation of this kind of study. Therefore, some of the methodology and ground rules for the study were developed as it was undertaken, so the book should be seen as the publication of work in progress, rather than a polished and definitive position statement.

Certainly my own ideas continue to change and develop as the research and the model have been discussed more widely with others in social work edu-cation, and elsewhere. These changes, which are evident throughout the book, are themselves evidence of learning through reflection, and they exemplify how I have tried to construct increasingly complex models to explain my own experiences. There are direct parallels between my own learning processes and the development of methodology and models in the book. The excitement I feel about the work, and its more recent extensions, is to do with the opportunity this kind of qualitative evaluation gives for looking again at what is known, and commonplace, in the experience of professional education and training.

Any stage looks different when the lighting is varied: social work education certainly looks different from the perspectives of those involved in it, and whose stories comprise this study. A single spotlight might have thrown heavy shadows, and brought the events on stage into sharp relief – but it is the many and varied lights that those on stage use to illumine their own worlds that reveal the nuances and subtleties of their interactions.

This study is about the anatomy of supervision – dissecting the processes of teaching and learning; and, when the component features have been identified, re-building them into new and different models and theories. In time, I hope that this study may be seen as a step along the road to establishing a *paradigm of learning* in professional and vocational education and training.

Derek Gardiner

Acknowledgements

This book owes a debt to many people for their help and encouragement. Dr Roy Cox supervised the doctoral work on which the book is based, and I am particularly indebted to him for his unwavering support during the uneven progress of part-time study. His colleagues, especially David Warren Piper and Dr Robert Murray, at the Centre for Higher Education Studies, provided a base which was much appreciated.

The Central Council for Education and Training in Social Work allowed study leave for one afternoon per week for two academic years, and then fifteen days towards writing up the thesis. Some of my colleagues there have been both stimulating and supportive, and read drafts of various parts of the thesis. I am grateful for the contributions of Andrew Cornwell and Dr Peter Mathias. The latter has also contributed substantially to the subsequent refinement and extension of the model developed in this research.

Elsewhere in social work education I have been equally fortunate. Professor Robert Harris has encouraged my involvement with the professional journals, and we have discussed the implications of this study over many years. Douglas Badger, Colin Whittington and Jenny Gray have all published work which has debated and developed the ideas contained in the early published accounts of this research. Jenny Gray's work was particularly useful in the development of the model of learning during the study; and she has helped in the task of turning a Ph.D. thesis written for a few people into a book directed at a wider audience.

The debt to those who took part in the study, and who gave generously of their time, interest, and ideas is enormous. The need for confidentiality prevents naming the supervisors and students who made the largest commitment – those in the single case study in Chapter 3, and those who appear as case illustrations in Chapters 5 and 6.

My wife, Fiona Gardiner, has borne the burden of a job and running a household with even less help than usual, yet has always provided the supportive environment necessary for a part-time student (and part-time author) to devote energy to work, to the research, and to writing.

Usually, there is acknowledgement of the contribution of a loyal typist who struggled with many drafts. However, the advent of word-processing software for micro-computers has meant that the book was written and typed by the author. Therefore, all errors are my own. Similarly, there is the usual disclaimer that views expressed in this book are my own, and not necessarily those of CCETSW.

1

Introduction

1.1 Background to the study

This book is about *quality* – quality in student learning, quality in teaching, and quality in social work education as a whole. It is also about finding and developing *methods of evaluating quality*, especially to explore how students and supervisors actually teach and learn in supervision. The book is based on a research study undertaken for a higher degree (Gardiner 1987c). It is a substantially revised (and shorter) version of the doctoral thesis, excluding a good deal of the methodological discussion, and the justification of the focus and approach.

For many years social work courses have been criticized for their perceived lack of relevance to current practice (CCETSW 1977), with particular concerns being expressed about the half of the course spent in practice placements. Recently, the validating body, the Central Council for Education and Training in Social Work (CCETSW 1987), in bidding for funds to extend courses to a minimum of three years, asserted that:

> There is growing evidence that . . . current education and training arrangements can no longer routinely equip social workers with the knowledge and skills they need . . . [and that] The CQSW has suffered from a shortage of good learning experiences for students on their practice placements.

Central Government turned down this bid, but in doing so acknowledged the importance of improving the quality of practice placements in raising overall standards. The DHSS (now the Department of Health) has provided funds intended to improve standards of practice learning within existing training programmes.

Whilst this book is directly relevant to these developments, it is not written simply in response to them, because the study was intended to consider how to improve the quality of student learning regardless of the length of courses.

The period during which the research was undertaken saw the higher education system, and professional training programmes, subjected to resource constraints and increasing public scrutiny. Media attention given to success-ive crises made the quality of basic grade staff a matter of concern beyond social work itself. These changes have produced increasing demands for explicitness, and definition of the purposes of training programmes. The lobby for competency-based, and vocationally-relevant training has led to, and been stimulated by, the establishment of a National Council for Vocational Qualifications.

In the same period, there have also been shifts in validation and accreditation strategies for professional and higher education programmes, with moves towards increased self-monitoring and evaluation within institutions and departments. These moves have been in response to demands that higher education should demonstrate 'fitness for purpose', and that professionals should be equipped for practice at the end of their training.

Research into higher education over the last decade has reflected a shift away from studies which measured the quantifiable aspects of educational activity, towards evaluating qualitative elements of the educational process – specifically in relation to the nature and quality of student learning. Practitioner-research is seen as having an important part to play in educational evaluation.

For the twenty years or so before this study began, social work education paid relatively little attention to teaching and learning in practice placements. Instead there was concentration on the content of the academic disciplines which social work students studied during their training. This was so not only in relation to the published literature, but also in relation to the focus of course requirements made by the validating body. Changes in those requirements at the beginning of the 1980s specified areas of students' knowledge and abilities which had to be demonstrated. These changes concerning student assessment went alongside more explicit expectations that educational institutions and agencies should work closely together in course planning, in the selection and assessment of students, and in relation to the practice component of the course.

Social work courses are essentially concerned with adults' learning, yet explicitness about teaching and learning (in curriculum materials submitted in the validation process) borrows heavily from traditional, hierarchical models of teaching. Developments in conceptualizing teaching and learning processes for adult learners have failed to penetrate very far into professional and vocational education – although they have relevance and, potentially, great value (Newble and Entwistle 1986). Despite the centrality of the placements in developing practice competence for social workers, there have been very few research-based studies of teaching and learning in supervision so the validating body, course planners, and social work teachers have been hampered in attempts to improve the quality of practice learning.

The research study on which this book is based was a beginning attempt to develop a grounded theory (Glaser and Strauss 1967) of teaching and learning for professional competence. It is intended to contribute to developmental work to improve qualifying training for social workers, but it also has implications for other kinds of professional and vocational preparation.

Attention in this study is directed to the experience of supervision from the perspectives of those involved. It seeks to describe and to interpret those experiences; then it attempts to recognize patterns in such data, and to systematize them into a model which can account for patterns in the inter-actions which demonstrably occur in individual supervision sessions and in placements as a whole. This requires the development and extension of qualitative methodologies in educational research; it also draws upon recent findings from research into student learning in higher education in many countries.

The research reported in this study is innovative in focus, approach and results. It is presented in a form which allows others to see clearly how the study developed, the legitimation for its nature, and the validity for its perspectives and findings. Whilst it may contribute to the development of qualitative methodologies in educational evaluation, and to the formulation of further research and evaluation of professional and vocational education, that is not the primary purpose of this book. The book is, however, intended to help students, supervisors, tutors, and policy-makers to understand the teaching and learning processes in supervision by providing an anatomy of the supervisory process, and new ways to understand teaching and learning interactions directed at improving professional competence.

1.2 An outline of the book

The research is reported in chronological order, to show how the focus and methods used were refined in the light of the findings as the study developed. **Chapter 2** reviews the supervision literature, and identifies a 'classical model' of casework supervision which still influences current supervisory practice. Some brief accounts of the author's own experiences in social work education illustrate the pervasive impact of the model. The main features of this classical model are identified, and the aims of the present research study are expressed in terms of the limitations of that model. The rest of the chapter summarizes some methodological issues raised by the study. The literature on qualitative evalua-tion is considered, and a rationale for using a range of qualitative methods is described.

Chapter 3 reports the first phase of data collection, and describes the major themes and issues to emerge. The first part was an open-ended questionnaire exercise intended to explore how experienced supervisors learnt and taught, and the problems they had in supervision with some kinds of students. The second part was an in-depth case study of supervision of an entire placement carried out by tape-recording the sessions. It became clear from these two exercises that students' and supervisors' approaches to learning were important in explaining what had occurred, especially the patterns of interaction in the supervisory relationship.

Chapter 4 reviews the relevant adult learning research literature, and considers how some of this work from Sweden, Britain and the United States could contribute to conceptualizing teaching and learning processes in super-vision. Particular attention is given to work on learning styles and to stages of development for adult learners. Subsequent data collection is planned in the light of this work, and of the findings from the first phase of the study.

Chapters 5 and 6 present, as descriptive case studies, the findings of the major data collection phase in the study. The patterns of interaction between supervisors and students are identified, and some generalizations of the patterns are developed from the case examples. In **Chapter 7** these elements are developed more systematically and a preliminary model, which describes and accounts for the interactive patterns, is developed. It consists of three levels of interaction between students and supervisors, derived from their conceptions of (and expectations of), the learning process itself. Some building blocks for a new paradigm of learning in social work education are described in the context of research into adult learning published whilst this study was being undertaken and written up.

Chapter 8 identifies some implications for social work education, and for other professional and vocational preparation, which emerge from the study. The subsequent development and extension of the model, and further work prompted by the study are briefly described. The book is concluded by a summary and overview of the research.

2

The Limitations of Traditional
Approaches to Supervision

2.1   The classical literature

Writing about supervision in the United Kingdom has been heavily influenced
by the American social casework supervision literature.

The *practice* of social work in the UK has diversified substantially since the
introduction of generic agencies and generic training. The *practice* literature can
be seen as a reaction to social casework approaches which are, in essence, a
psycho-social, dynamic interaction between two unequal participants, with the
purpose of helping the client's social adjustment through emotional growth.

The changes in practice approach challenge various aspects of the casework
model: by extending the number of practitioners (e.g. working in teams), or the
number of clients (e.g. working with groups, working with families) or by
changing the interventive processes in which the social worker is engaged (e.g.
to include advocacy and other indirect work on behalf of the client). These
changes produce different explanations of client behaviour, different patterns of
service delivery, and differences in the power relationship between worker and
client. Challenges to the casework paradigm have come from a radical-political
perspective (e.g. Illich 1970; Illich *et al.* 1977), from family therapy (e.g.
Minuchin 1974), systems theory (e.g. Pincus and Minahan 1973), from patch-
based approaches (e.g. Hadley 1984), and in residential work (e.g. Hudson
1984).

Despite these developments of the conceptual base of social work *practice*, the
social work *education* literature continues to be dominated by models derived
from the traditional one-to-one model of social casework.

For the purposes of this study, it was decided to identify the key features of one
of the most influential of the British texts, and to trace the roots of the model in
the earlier British and American contributions cited. The influence of these
works on later contributions to the literature is also described.

The text chosen is by Young (1967), whose book on student supervision was
published not long before she took up the post of Director of CCETSW. She
continued in that post until the end of 1986, so her ideas were at the centre of
policy debates and discussions for over twenty years. The major features of her
model seem to be:

1. that there is a hierarchical relationship between teacher and learner,
2. that there is a body of theory, learned in college which is to be applied in practice,
3. that all students' learning will have specific arrival points and paths of discovery and these will not be distinguished for individual students,
4. that a naive, inexperienced student is taught by an experienced, expert teacher,
5. that there are right answers and right ways to do things,
6. that assessment involves only the teacher, who evaluates the progress of the student towards the required position.

There are a number of important features of any educational model which may be implicit in writings about its operation. However, in this literature the authors are admirably explicit. The essential elements of this model of professional educational process will be considered in turn.

The relationship between teacher and learner is hierarchical, as Young sees it (emphases are added, throughout this section):

> *The personal relationship* which is established between the individual student and his supervisor . . . must be based on the *acceptance by both the people involved that one is in the role of teacher and the other a learner.*
>
> The student knows that *the supervisor has this authority* . . . if both of them accept this fact and the inevitable difference in status which it brings, *it will leave the supervisor more free to teach and the student to learn.*

It is possible to show how Young sees the relationship of college-based teaching to field practice:

> Field work placements provide experience of a live situation, in which *the student can apply his theoretical knowledge* (of organization and structure) . . . *in the same way as he tests out the casework teaching in the classroom against his experience with his own clients.*
>
> The *knowledge which the student must be able to apply in practice* will be in three main areas . . .

In this model, there are specific destinations, known to the teacher, and there are specific ways of reaching them:

> A supervisor must help a student towards the first, and probably tentative, '*arrival point*', and throughout the case will hold him to continuing along '*the path of discovery*'.

All new supervisors, like students, are assumed to be naive:

> . . . [new] supervisors tend to provide the student with work, and to offer some advice and guidance gleaned from their own experiences, but *have only vague ideas about what the student has to learn, and even less definite plans about what they have to teach.*

Control and ownership of the learning process, and the assessment process, rests firmly with the teacher:

> The student who is *made to think for himself*, from the very beginning of his training . . .
>
> The written report . . . must be the responsibility of the supervisor, and opinions vary as to whether the student should be given the document to read . . . The supervisor must give an honest assessment of the student's performance, even when there is a risk of discouraging the student . . . *Occasionally a student will ask for a copy of his evaluation to keep. Before a supervisor agrees to this, the course tutor should be consulted* . . .

Problems in supervision are thought to derive from 'anxiety' on the part of the student or supervisor:

Common *Anxieties*

1. . . . *One of the common anxieties* among students and new supervisors is . . .
2. The client's reaction . . . this perhaps has something to do with *the implied anxiety* sometimes expressed that a client will suffer if the worker changes . . .
3. The supervisor's uncertainties . . . *This anxiety* sometimes results in a new supervisor feeling . . .

These points amply demonstrate not only specific components of the model, but also (perhaps even more importantly) the *use of language and terminology derived from the practice of social casework with clients* to describe what happens in the supervision relationship between supervisors and students.

The literature of the period includes many debates about whether supervision is actually therapy, or whether it should be. This debate is related to the psychotherapy literature of the time, and has resurfaced recently in the literature on supervision in family therapy training, which is undertaken by social workers (amongst others) and is taught by many who had first trained as social workers twenty or more years ago. This preoccupation with questions of 'isomorphism' between the teaching system and the client system is demonstrated in a recent dissertation at the Institute for Family Therapy which discusses the family therapy literature (Gray 1986):

> Liddle and Saba (1983) discuss the principle of the isomorphic nature of training and therapy, which specifies that 'form, pattern, content, affect are recursively replicated in the inter-related domains of training and therapy'. They suggest that trainers would do well to understand and to intentionally utilise with their trainees the same basic principles of change employed in therapy . . . They also suggest that 'over-emphasis . . . of the isomorphic relationship could lead to the erroneous conclusion that training is simply therapy with one's students'.

Young expresses a debt to a number of authors, including Garrett (1954), Deed (1962), Howarth (1961), Towle (1954), Austin (1952), and Heywood (1964).

She points the reader to their work for further study. By following this suggestion, one can explore in more detail how a number of key features (of terminology, educational model, focus, and purpose) of Young's model of supervision have been shaped.

The paper by Deed was one of a series of contributions about training in the (British) Journal *Case Conference* in 1962. The author reflects on her long experience of supervising, which started before the second world war. Of particular relevance is the explicit way she describes moving from assuming that *all* students were essentially the same to distinguishing different learning needs (determined by the type of course they were on). At first, she says:

> I thought, as everyone else did at the time, in terms of 'students' without attaching any particular labels to them relating to the stage of their training or to the kind of course they were taking . . . I assumed they all came to me to learn roughly the same kind of things . . . neither I nor the tutor thought in terms of different stages of learning, nor of degree, or certificate, or post-graduate course.

She goes on to explain that *stage* meant the difference between taking a pre-professional or a professional course:

> As a result of this distinction students in the first group, no matter whether they were taking degree or certificate courses, were thought of as being at a much earlier stage of training than the second group.

She cautions against making too rigid a distinction between the stages, and describes a 'natural but continuous growth of learning' which is related to the type of course the student is on.

Deed makes no other distinctions between the students, and, indeed, explicitly generalizes about *all* students by the use of the terms 'they', 'their' and 'them' in an undifferentiated account of 'their' learning:

> *All students* . . . enter their first placement with great enthusiasm but with some naivity . . . *Their need at this stage* is to do rather than to observe as soon as possible. *They do not know enough* to observe intelligently or to appreciate what a good caseworker is doing when she sees her clients . . . *The student's first need is* . . . *His learning at this stage consists of* . . .

She goes on to describe the problems she and her colleagues ran into when the first group of students were finishing a seventeen-month course:

> Up till this final six months in the field *he has been able to remain intellectual in approach and he is unused to thinking and speculating imaginatively about actual individual people* [sic] . . . *still able to make foolish and unexpected mistakes which we normally do not expect at such a late stage of training* . . .
>
> . . . but in spite of all these fears . . . all made good use of the final placement . . . but they were a puzzle to their supervisors in the penultimate stage. This may well have been our fault . . . These post-graduates did not fit to our accustomed labels and *supervisors were obliged to consider each*

one very individually . . . [and] *allow for the differences between students taking different courses.*

The material presented by Deed is revealing. Because she seems to recognize students' different learning needs only by her definitions of stage (from the type of courses they are on), she sees problems occurring when students behave in ways which are different from the teachers' expectations of how they should be learning. There seems to be little recognition that this lack of understanding of individual differences might be why the supervisors had such difficulties.

The Deed paper is also explicit about other key elements of casework supervision, including the relationship between theory and practice:

> During this *they are taught all the theory they will ever get* . . . and they also get the only opportunities they will have as students *to apply this theory in practice* under supervision.

In her account of the model (like Young's), theory is taught by teachers, in college, to students who will apply it, in practice situations in agencies. There is no recognition that students (and indeed workers) might need to build up generalizations from their own practice to generate practice wisdom (Hardiker and Barker 1981) or to transfer that learning to other, different practice situations which they will meet in their professional lifetime (Gardiner 1984b).

To Deed, and Young, teachers are the experts, the repositories of theory, and the student begins as an empty vessel. Deed describes this naive student:

> He has, as yet, no theory and very little knowledge of social legislation or the social services and . . . though relatively mature after three or four years in a University, *his maturity is not likely to stand up well to some of the experiences he meets in social work.* Intellectual in approach, he is unlikely to have foreseen how his own feelings and attitudes will be involved.
>
> It can be really harmful when the student, thrilled and excited by this new experience for which he is ill-prepared, cannot stop looking at himself and his own motives to the extent that he, or she, *comes very near to a nervous breakdown* [sic].

This last point, besides emphasizing the educational model being used, further demonstrates the parallels between supervision and therapy. Another of the articles referred to by Young is by Howarth (1961), where, in a paper intended to be an introduction to casework supervision, she also takes up this isomorphism issue:

> The understanding and use of personal relationship, both in casework and in supervision is here taken to be fundamental to the purpose of social workers in whatever setting they have chosen to work. If individuals are to be helped solve their problems, or students aided in learning to practise casework, it is best achieved within a constructive relationship. *The two situations are different, but sufficiently alike to cause misunderstanding and difficulty* . . .

Turning to the ways in which students learn in supervision there is the perennial question of whether casework is therapy . . . The methods of supervision must have a good deal in common with those of casework; there are also important differences but there is no need to stress these if the value of the similarities is appreciated . . . *The ways in which teachers behave with their students cannot be basically dissimilar to their casework behaviour* . . . The student is, however, always different from a client. He is preparing to perform an honourable part in a profession and he brings a strength of purpose and a wealth of experience to the task . . . learning to be a caseworker demands that a student should himself change and he *may sometimes feel as bewildered and anxious as he perceives his client to be.*

Austin (1952) makes clear the roots of this continuing debate in a further paper cited by Young:

Social work has drawn on psychoanalytic theory. The contributions of Freud and his followers . . . have been incorporated into social work teaching as well as into practice.

American psychiatric social workers originally used psychiatrists and psycho-analysts as their supervisors – until there was a sufficient number of trained social workers to begin to take on the task themselves. This is well demon-strated in the American texts to which Young refers (Garrett 1954; Towle 1954 and more recently, Suboda 1986). Garrett's book has an introduction by a psychiatrist which includes the following:

It is of comparatively minor importance to cite that the present individual supervisor-student method of instruction is but a reactivation of the old *physician-medical student apprenticeship system or that it has borrowed heavily from the more modern psychoanalyst-analytic control student approach.* The fact remains that this device . . . *has been brought to its highest order of excellence by educators in social work.*

As might be expected, Garrett emphasizes the same relation of theory to practice described earlier:

But professional people whose life's work is the *application of knowledge to real persons* . . . must acquire knowledge in the richer and more vital sense: Skill in *applying abstract theory to the complexities of practice* in a way which will produce the desired results . . . *theory is learned in the first instance in the classroom* . . . but under able supervision the student comes to experience the exhilaration that comes from *recognizing in field work individual examples of what has been learned in class.*

Garrett here assumes that 'knowledge' is 'applied to real persons', and seems to see it as synonymous with 'abstract theory', which is seen as a set of generaliz-ations the student must apply to particular situations. The key element is that the generalizations do not come from the student's own experience, but from someone else. They are not owned by the student; they belong to the teacher, who will instruct the student in their 'application'. The making, and ownership, of generalizations from practice is a theme explored later.

Like Deed, Garrett has a sense of stages or rates of development, though she equally does not distinguish between students except in so far as they differ from her expectations of normal progress:

> [The faculty supervisor] may see that some of the student's needs are being neglected . . . she may notice in other areas the student is being pushed ahead too rapidly and may suggest a slow-down . . .

This shows that Garrett has a view about what is too fast or too slow, although she does not offer criteria designed to judge it by. Instead, she goes on to describe her view of learning difficulties:

> Together she [the faculty supervisor] and the supervisor may achieve *insight into the emotional difficulties through which the student is working* and thus help to *overcome blockings which stand in the way of further growth.*

Again, learning is equated with the emotional growth of the student, and learning problems are the fault of the student's assumed emotional difficulties.

It is worth reflecting on what some of this might mean for the teacher-learner relationship: students are expected to learn in a particular way (in supervision, using the supervisor both as an instructor-teacher, and in a way which at least parallels how clients use workers); and at a particular rate (determined not by them, but by the college-based teacher). If they do not match these expectations of others, they are assumed to have some emotional difficulties which are causing them to go too quickly or too slowly.

Individual variations in a student's learning, for Garrett, are not variations to do with style or stage of learning, nor of motivation and ability:

> But as these individual differences come to light, some *hinted* between the lines, others *more or less concealed*, either *consciously or unconsciously* in original material. Knowledge of these individual variations is gained slowly and often can be *discovered only by painstaking diagnosis* . . .

The use of language and concepts here is striking – 'hinted', 'concealed', 'consciously or unconsciously', 'painstaking diagnosis'. Similarly, Austin (1952), in considering the factors to be taken into account in making 'an educational diagnosis' suggests:

> . . . evaluating the *nature and degree of his anxiety* and *the capacity of the ego to master anxiety* and to engage in creative learning . . .
>
> *Defenses* – their character as well as their fluidity – offer important clues to a preliminary educational diagnosis.
>
> Because considerable range and variation in ability to learn exist within any pattern of behaviour, *a differential diagnosis* is important.

Austin here is talking about what to do routinely in relation to *all* students; she is not only suggesting what should be done with students who have demonstrable learning problems, or whose performance is marginal.

Garrett and Austin are both talking about the relationship between the supervisor and the student, not about the therapist and the client. The use of such language and concepts reinforces the notion of isomorphism, but it does more as well. It also confirms the extent to which the language of the psycho-analytic consulting room has taken over what is happening in social work supervision.

It is helpful to consider this problem as one of *concept-leakage* from the practice situation into the teaching and learning context. It could be said that *concept-leakage lies at the heart of the classical paradigm of supervision in social work education*. It did not happen by chance – it was explicitly believed that the processes were essentially similar or that differences didn't matter (Howarth 1961) and that learning would come about as a result of the close matching of the therapeutic process with supervision.

Without a recognition of concept-leakage, how else should one read the earlier quotations from this literature, and then Garrett's description of the role of the faculty supervisor (the college tutor, in Britain), where the students apparently do not have responsibility for making sense of experience, in their own individual way?

> The faculty supervisor's role is to be certain that the supervisor-student relationship is operating at its maximum as an enabling process to further the student's professional learning. She *senses blockings on either side, sorts out reality and transference situations*, and directs her attention toward *converting the student's experiences into constructive learning*.

Garrett's book is divided into sections to describe what should be covered in each of the termly visits of the tutor to the agency, which reinforce the notion that *all students go through the same stages at the same time*:

> *Beginning students are characteristically involved in emancipation problems . . . They are struggling in the marriage versus career dilemma . . .* Since the way they eventually solve these conflicts often bears a direct relationship to their success as a caseworker, they come up for consideration on each successive visit . . .

> [In the Winter visit] . . . the primary factor that is involved . . . is, however, the fact that *both students and their cases are now arriving at the point* where more than beginning skills are needed . . . *the student . . . becomes frustrated and discouraged . . . She tends to belittle the skills she has acquired . . .*

> [The Spring visit] . . . *almost all students now show miraculous progress . . . the finishing student has acquired* a method of self-study so that she can proceed to minimise her weaknesses and develop her strengths . . .

> [About assessment] Supervisors sometimes take on the student's discouragement and wonder whether she will ever become a caseworker. Forty nine times out of fifty, she will; but *the forty nine students are usually sure*

they are the fiftieth, and the fiftieth is the least aware that there is any question about her performance, even when it has been repeatedly discussed with her.

There is a certainty pervading this literature that there is a right way to go about things, and the teaching task is to instruct (all) students how to do things in this right way. Garrett also gives a detailed account of how she sees student-supervisor problems:

As a student becomes more deeply involved in psychological material, she often becomes unable to see her supervisor as a real person . . . The degree of emotion and a personal emphasis in her discussion *reveal the degree of her transference manifestation . . . [students'] complaints usually centre on her [the supervisor's] method of working with them, thus revealing their desire to have her gratify all of their needs.*

If students wish to learn in their own way, or for the teacher to teach in a way which might match this, the students are 'revealing their desire to have her gratify all of their needs'. In other words, it would be seen as a learning pathology. However, Garrett acknowledges:

Students have an uncanny way of sensing or uncovering a supervisor's *weak spots.* There is often an *element of truth in a student's complaint,* although her feelings may be *highly exaggerated projections.*

Thus, students may be right in challenging how they are taught, but this again is described in terms which echo the problems of clients. Alternatively, it may be the supervisor's fault which the tutor has to deal with. In this way, the hierarchical relationship of therapist and patient is super-imposed not only onto the student-supervisor relationship, but also onto the tutor-supervisor interaction as well. This hierarchy of hierarchies also has its roots in psychoanalytic training, and is still taken as the model of choice in psychoanalytic, and in family therapy, training (Gray 1986):

The role of the supervisor-of-supervision in the therapeutic or training system . . . The hierarchical nature and structure of the relationship between consultation, supervision and therapy (Burnham and Harris 1985) has been described. They have developed a schema which addresses the multi-level nature of supervision and consultation.

Almost all writers in this classical literature on casework refer to the work of Towle (1954). Indeed Young (1967) describes it as a 'standard work on the subject . . . (which) repays careful study, but for practical purposes, most fieldwork teachers will find it too long and detailed (sic).' Not surprisingly, Towle articulates (and may be the source of) many of the points identified above:

. . . I can honestly say that *when I turned my hand to teaching social work I was consciously using largely my psycho-analytically oriented casework learning . . .*

. . . it has become clear that some of the *initial anxiety* in social work learning stems from not knowing rather than from the threat of change implied in learning . . . *He [the student] is frequently helpless, confused, and fearful out of the lack of the know-what, know-how, and know-why* . . . at such moments he feels helpless . . .

. . . the essential differences between client and student . . . have been first, that the client does not recognise social casework treatment as a learning process, even though, when skilfully conducted, it is one . . . *The needs and wants which drive a client* to seek help are seen and felt as 'a problem' . . . In contrast to a problem, *the needs and wants that motivate the student* are seen, felt, and regarded by others as a goal.

For Towle, then, the process is essentially similar for clients and students, although there is a further hierarchical distinction – between students and clients. Clients are 'driven' by 'a problem' but students are 'motivated' towards a 'goal'. She also introduces the remarkable notion of the 'uneducable (sic) student':

> . . . *if the student is rigid in defending his point of view when instructor and colleagues take issue with him, serious question as to his educability arises . . . perhaps he persists in fitting facts into theory rather than applying theory to facts.*

Leaving aside, for the moment, questions about what are 'facts' and who determines what is 'fact', there are clearly specified things to learn, and it is not expected that students will challenge their instructor's views about these. If students persist in asserting their own divergent views, and try to build their own practice theory, they run the risk of being seen as rigid and uneducable. Not only is there a single right way in this model, but all such diversity is frowned upon.

These American authors contribute clear and explicit accounts of how they see the supervision process. Reading them thirty or more years later raises questions about these assumptions and assertions. But their influence on the British literature is undoubted. Even when making allowances for the subtle shifts in meaning across the Atlantic, and through time, there can be little doubt of their continuing impact. Heywood (1964), a British social work tutor, dedicates her book 'To Charlotte Towle, a great and beloved teacher':

> Supervision means giving knowledge quickly and as fully as the student can understand. Before seeing a case the student should be well-briefed in everything he needs to know to get started: what the situation is; what difficulties may be expected to arise and why; how such difficulties may be handled.

There is one further area of work in this literature which is of interest in the present study; both Young and Towle allude to it: how students learn to practise in situations which are different from those in which their learning arose. In other words, how students transfer their learning from the context in which it arose to other situations in which they will be called on to intervene during their professional careers. The model described in the literature, of applying theory to practice, does not easily account for students generalizing from their own experiences, and beginning to learn how they learn. This issue is developed, in some detail, later.

2.2 An overview of the classical literature

In taking an overview of this classical literature, it is immediately obvious that there is little direct reporting of what actually occurs in supervision. Interpretations of events are described at such a level of generality that individual differences between supervisors and students are largely ignored, and the expectation of the learning process is essentially the same for all students.

It is also evident that most of the contributions are from college-based teachers, not those who are currently involved in supervision, and that these contributions are overlaid with the implicit hierarchical relationship between tutors and supervisors. The descriptions of the supervision process are couched in the language, concepts and terminology of social casework practice. The activity of supervision has two main components: one, instruction and direct teaching of social work 'theory'; the other is the emotional growth of the student in ways which at least parallel, if not directly replicate, the therapeutic relationship in casework practice – which leads to a continuing preoccupation with whether supervision *is* therapy.

Identifying the features of the dominant paradigm and making them explicit may not, at this stage, be giving a full account of the model. The lack of a full account does not prevent significant influence on those in the field, as Kuhn (1970) makes clear:

> [Scientists can] agree in their identification of a paradigm without agreeing on, or attempting to produce, a full interpretation or rationalisation of it. Lack of a standard interpretation . . . will not prevent a paradigm from guiding research.

Kuhn describes how the identification of anomaly can challenge existing theories and interpretations in the natural sciences, and can lead to the establishment of other frames of explanation than those previously existing in a discipline. These anomalies can be either (or both) of the following. One kind could lead to the refutation of a theory – for example, if theory held that all swans in the world are white, the finding of a single black swan would refute the theory. The second kind of anomaly is one which would challenge the dominant paradigm which underlies all prevailing theories in an area of study.

Thus, the existence of assumptions which do not explicate experiences in supervision should lead to close inspection of the limitations of the dominant paradigm. The classical supervision model purports to describe educational processes and activities, but it does so by using explanations derived from a practice paradigm. This need not be in itself a disadvantage. However in the present case, a number of the major features of the *paradigm of teaching and of practice* are unhelpful and may conflict with attempts to value the contribution of students to supervision, and to take responsibility for their own learning.

The prime feature of the practice paradigm is concept-leakage, which underlies the assumptions and features of the classical model:

1. *student learning is synonymous with emotional growth;*
2. the *focus is on individuals rather than on the interactions between them;*
3. *problems are seen and described as pathologies* in the growth and development of individuals;
4. there is *a hierarchical, traditional teacher-learner relationship* and a similar pattern is *replicated in the relative status of tutors and supervisors;*
5. there is an emphasis on *the authority of the discipline* itself, and *what* is taught, *rather than on how students learn;*
6. *the practice arena is seen as an illustration* of college-based teaching, and an *opportunity to apply previous instruction in practice;*
7. *students are assumed to be relatively homogenous* in style and stage of learning, so no account is taken of individual differences between teachers and learners;
8. there are *no significant differences between teachers in HOW they teach.*

Implied in these assumptions is the belief that there is a right way to do social work and a right way to supervise, as well as a right path which students must follow in order to become competent practitioners. This 'right path' moves from an assumed naive, immature student to a professional worker through a maturation process. There is an expectation of generating and dealing with the anxieties of the student by an activity which parallels social casework with clients.

It is possible to discern, in this classical literature, some further concept-leakage – from traditional models of education which have a number of similar features to social casework practice. These include a hierarchical relationship between teachers and learners (with considerable role distance between them), together with valuing of the expertise residing in the teacher and the discipline rather than students and their experience.

In summary, then, one can describe the traditional approach to *supervision as a paradigm of practice, and of teaching (i.e. instruction)* rather than a *paradigm of education, and of learning.*

2.3   Supervision literature since the classical period

Since the works discussed above, relatively little substantial work on supervision has appeared in the British literature. What has falls into two main categories: those which are largely derivative of the traditions and work identified above; and other work on the practice component of qualifying training.

Those publications which are derivative of the classical model include Danbury (1979 and 1986), Kent (1969), and Pettes (1979). Their inclusion within the classical tradition is readily demonstrable. Kent devotes the major part of her book to reproducing, then commenting upon, the written record which a supervisor had made after each supervision session with a particular student. She also reproduces some of the student's notes of his work with clients. It seems that Kent is acting as supervisor-of-supervision during this placement, and evidence is given of her relationship with the supervisor through the latter's records. There are no records of the student's experience of supervision, nor are there any direct quotations of the interaction in the supervision sessions. Kent refers directly to Towle, Heywood, and Young. Two indicative quotations demonstrate her reliance on the assumptions and language of the traditional model (emphases are added, throughout this section):

> Thus the (beginning) student social worker *usually needs help and support initially* so he is able to take the plunge . . . Initially . . . *he is self-conscious and uneasy* in interviews, *constantly trying to assess whether he is doing the 'right' or 'wrong' thing*, and *driven by his anxiety to activity and talking . . . His anxiety at the start* may cause him to appear more competent than he is, he may initially resist making use of the supervisor or become over-dependent . . . he *begins to develop some slight capacity to look at himself objectively and critically in the casework situation.*

Kent perpetuates the assumption that all students are the same, and that all students will begin as incompetent, and immature. However, more than half of all social work students have at least two years' experience in paid social work jobs before entering training courses and less than a quarter of social work students have no paid experience and begin training as new entrants (Gardiner 1985). Generalizations about all students being immature and inexperienced are likely to be problematic today.

Pettes, in a 1979 revision of her earlier (1967) text writes in terms which American social work educators thirty years before would recognize:

> *Supervision may be described as one of the many methods or processes in social work.* To describe supervision thus . . . will avoid the old fear of *supervision as an attempt to 'casework the caseworker'.*
>
> *Nearly all students are anxious* . . . Sometimes anxiety may be masked by apparent complacency, and *the supervisor may need to point out deficiencies in order to bring the anxiety to the surface, or to arouse sufficient anxiety to stimulate learning.*

It is not surprising, then, that Pettes also refers to Towle, Young, and Kent. Similarly, Danbury (1979) is concerned about the student's anxiety, and the prime purpose of supervision seems to help to cope with it.

Turning to the other main work on placements (as well as this neo-classical group) they can readily be divided between those published by the validating body, and the rest. CCETSW has published four contributions: a report on student units in social work education (Curnock 1975), a research report into practice placements (Syson and Baginsky 1981), a study of the structure and content of CQSW courses (Casson 1982), and a Workshop Report (CCETSW 1983).

The first of these, by Curnock, is a survey of the role of student units. There is no section on teaching and learning processes, and only a small element of the survey considers the content focus of supervision sessions. The Syson and Baginsky study provides a further example of concept-leakage, since although neither of the authors has practised nor trained as social workers, the research report is couched in the terms of casework practice and casework supervision. The authors were evidently looking for the issues which recur in the classical literature:

> The role of therapist was not acceptable to nearly all practice teachers. However, while the use of therapy might relate to the student's own problems and be considered outside the scope of the placement, *discussion of 'feelings' was regarded by most supervisors and many tutors as a legitimate and desirable focus of discussion.* Confusion as to which feelings supervisors were wishing to discuss may have existed.
>
> *Whether or not a supervisor took a therapeutic role towards the student*, differences in viewpoint or values could affect the content of the discussion, particularly in the placements where one of the parties was psycho-analytically oriented but the other was not . . . [In one case] the student then had to decide whether to try a supportive, psycho-analytic or a social learning approach according to whether the client was dim, depressed or simply lazy. She disliked her supervisor's interpretation.
>
> *It is not of course necessary to be friends in order to discuss feelings*, but a fairly relaxed, comfortable relationship is essential.

We see here Syson echoing the language of social caseworkers in her descriptive accounts of supervision. She also has an expectation, like those she quotes (Towle, Young, Pettes) that there are right answers, and proper ways to do things so she looks for them:

> *The proper relationship between the student and supervisor* was difficult for some to define, and in a few cases, to establish.

The concept-leakage is particularly interesting here, since the qualitative methodology (and a researcher who was not herself a social worker) could have allowed a different interpretative frame to be developed. She makes a brief reference to styles of supervision, which includes accessibility of the supervisor to the student. She considers how to get deeper material, and recognizes that 'direct observation of relationships in a placement may be the only technique for obtaining such information.' That is precisely what is undertaken in the present study.

The Casson study represents the most substantial attempt to address developments in educational thinking and relate these to social work courses' content and structure. Although not intended to look at the practice component directly, there are many implications of the work which social work educators seem slow to respond to. Certainly, when it was published, it had a mixed reception, not least because of the unfamiliarity of the language and the concepts being used.

The final CCETSW publication in the field is perhaps misleadingly entitled *Research in Practice Teaching*, since it is in fact the report of a workshop intended to allow pairs of college- and agency-based teachers to develop the integration of their work by means of joint projects. None of the reported projects focuses on teaching and learning processes in supervision, although some do report progress in college-agency understanding and collaboration.

It is worth reflecting on the use of language and terminology in these areas. 'Practice teaching', 'Practice learning', 'Practice placements' are all terms used, but they are used in confusing ways, and sometimes (apparently) as synonyms. There is often confusion between *what* is to be learnt during the placement (if 'learning' is taken to be a noun) or *how* it is to be learnt (if 'learning' is taken to be a verb). Parsloe (1982) in an article entitled 'The Learning Process' makes no explicit reference to learning either as a noun or a verb.

In this study, the use of language and terminology was carefully considered. The term 'practice teaching' has generally been avoided – because an emphasis on *practice* and *teaching* is in danger of reinforcing the limitations of the classical model, and reinforcing concept-leakage. Thus the terms *supervisor* and *supervision* are used here.

Turning to the other literature, there are three elements: arrangements for placements; the assessment of students' performance; and the funding of placements. Only two contributions focus on the style or approach of supervisors. West (1984) uses a Jungian model of personality types to look at supervisory relationships which work, and those which do not. Michael (1976) describes styles of supervision which are essentially practice styles, rooted in the traditional model.

Since none of the other work is central to looking at the supervisory process, it is not considered in great detail here. It is sufficient to note that the two research-based contributions concern student assessment. One is a Masters thesis (Morrell 1979); the other is joint work between a research student and her academic supervisor (Brandon and Davies 1979). Practitioner-research (i.e. by those who are currently supervisors) in the field is largely absent from the published literature although some small scale activities are known to have been undertaken.

It is on the funding of supervision and practice placements that more supervisors have concentrated their attention. This is unsurprising in the present economic climate, with cuts in both higher education and the personal social services. Sawdon (1986) is the most substantial work here, and represents a well-marshalled defence of the funding of his student unit in a voluntary agency. His book describes his attempts to use the work of Knowles (1972 and 1978) in using an andragogical design for setting up placements, and in the general approach to supervision. None of the research on adult learning in Sweden or Britain is referenced in his work, and Sawdon is perhaps stronger on presage factors than the interactions of supervision. This is perhaps related to

Knowles' unfortunate tendency to prescription, since he does not always distinguish between approaches of individual learners (Knowles 1972):

> ... when working with mature people who are problem-centred in their orientation to learning ... they would see as much more relevant a curriculum that is organized around the problem areas with which social work deals, perhaps with a different but sequential set of problems each year ...

In the literature over more than forty years, what is most marked is the reliance on concepts leaked from the practice of social casework into accounts of the supervisory relationship. The literature does not show supervision sessions being recorded, teaching-learning interactions being reported, nor interviews with students and supervisors about how they construe the meaning of those events so there can be no direct challenge to the generalized, second hand, interpretations in that literature.

It may be, of course, that for some the isomorphism reflects a kind of metaphor of the transactions, which has somehow become reified (Gardiner 1972). Such dead metaphors, and their impact on learning, are described by Pratte (1981, in Tiberius 1986):

> a dead metaphor is one which we use as though it were literal ... Its inference is so shrouded in custom and habit, its comparison so covered over by the blind convention of everyday thinking that the metaphor controls what we think ... [it can] frequently obscure useful questions ... and force us to frame our investigations within unnecessary limits.

2.4   Three autobiographical accounts

It may be that concept-leakage in the classical model is a kind of dead metaphor which prevents a clear view of supervision. Some of my own experiences in social work education fall into this category, where the explanations offered by the classical model were unsatisfactory because they seemed partial, and potentially misleading. They are presented here as examples of what Kuhn (1970) would describe as challenges to the dominant paradigm within a discipline.

Being a social work student

In common with other students (Shaw and Walton 1978) my own experiences on placement were some of the most significant parts of the entire course. In my first practice placement I found supervision a strange and somewhat disturbing experience. There were apparently some rules, or expectations, which my supervisor seemed to take for granted, but which we were never able to make explicit in supervision.

My first social work placement was in a Child Guidance Clinic in a large provincial city. The approach in that clinic, like that of the social work course, was a traditional, psycho-dynamic one. My supervisor was, I believed, relatively inexperienced as a supervisor (having herself trained on the same course a short while before).

I considered that I needed to use the first placement to get broader experience of social work, and in particular to develop my practice skills in this milieu. I also wanted to begin to conceptualize my practice, because until then I had been working somewhat intuitively, with rather limited supervision.

My supervisor and I began to run into difficulties fairly early on in the placement because she seemed to believe that what I should write about in my reports, and talk to her about in supervision, were the feelings I had during and after the interviews. When I persisted in trying to focus on making sense of what was going on in the families I was working with, and between them and me in the interviews, it was assumed that I was 'being defensive', and that I had 'some block' about the expression of feelings which required the help of my supervisor to overcome.

The supervisor apparently found this situation very difficult, and this 'problem' had apparently been the subject of discussions in a group of tutors and new supervisors at the University. There were hints that I might be considered as a borderline student or might not pass the placement at all. I was highly motivated to pass the course, and felt very pressured by these events.

I recall getting angry at the suggestion that I might fail just because I apparently did not fit my supervisor's expectations of me: and when, later in the placement, I suggested that this anger had itself been an example of my ability to express feelings in the supervision sessions, the supervisor seemed pained and withdrawn.

After a particularly demanding episode with a client who had recently been bereaved (as I myself had also been), the supervision discussion seemed to bring enormous relief at first to my supervisor, who felt that at last I was 'getting into these feeling areas'. I insisted firmly that this was not the case, since I had been able to do that kind of work even before joining the course. As soon as I had challenged the assertion of an apparent change in my work being more to do with my supervisor's perceptions, and her limited evidence for such a view, she appeared to me to retreat again. These matters were never properly resolved.

With the benefit of hindsight it is possible to see that my supervisor and I had very different expectations about the appropriate use of supervision, which we never made explicit. I felt I was being treated like a client. My supervisor was apparently unsure of herself in what for her was a new and demanding role – but she presumably had clear expectations of what she saw as the 'right' way for supervision to be used. We did not seem to be engaged in the same enterprise – especially about who should be responsible for *my* learning.

Therefore, underlying these exchanges was a rather different but contributing dimension about power in educational relationships. Some teachers assume the role of experts, with a strong hierarchical flavour to their teaching. It is a seductive and potentially powerful position to believe that there are single right and wrong ways to understand and interpret the world – and it is threatening when others persist in not sharing or even challenging those assumptions (Gorer 1966):

> An important component in many schools of magic or esoteric knowledge is the employment of Words of Power; these Words give the user control over occult forces. For many people . . . some of the vocabulary of psychoanalysis and of general psychiatry . . . has acquired some of the characteristics of Words of Power. Many people appear to feel that when they have applied a psychoanalytic, or quasi-psychoanalytic term to a person or situation they have somehow gained control . . . (and) rendered it or him understandable, safe, innocuous.

Of course, it can be seen as a political act to attempt to take control of one's own learning. For students to try to do so can be a powerful challenge to the authority of teachers, perhaps especially new and inexperienced teachers.

In summary, it is evident that my supervisor and I were talking at cross purposes, and the frames of reference which we used were very different, with competing explanations of the events, especially in terms of *how* the teaching and learning would occur. However, the explanations which were attached to these experiences tended to locate cause, and responsibility (i.e. blame) with one person rather than seeing the mis-match of expectations as an *interactive* problem of construing meaning between the two of us. Some other frames of reference are more concerned with *meaning* than *cause*, as Rycroft makes clear in his reinterpretation of Freud's contribution to the study of interaction and communication (1966):

> What Freud did here was not to explain the patient's choice *causally* but to understand it and give it *meaning*, and the procedure he engaged in was not the scientific one of elucidating causes, but the semantic one of making sense of it. It can be argued here that Freud's work was really semantic . . . that neurotic symptoms are meaningful, disguised communications but . . . he formulated his findings in the conceptual framework of the physical sciences.

There is resonance with the intention of the present work to explore the meanings which students and supervisors attach to their experience of supervision.

Being a supervisor

When I later became a student supervisor, as a Student Unit Head, some of the issues raised in the literature review were very evident. The Unit at Thamesmead was unusual in two ways: first, it was not formally part of an agency, and acted as a small voluntary agency staffed mainly by students; second, it was established as part of an attempt to develop joint inter-

professional, community-based training for social workers, general practitioners, health visitors and others involved in community care (Adcock, Craig,
Gardiner, Jaques 1977; Jaques 1982; Gardiner 1984c).

The accounts here are derived from papers written at the time, and have the
advantage of not being altered by subsequent reinterpretation. A description of
the first period of the Unit's existence also reflects something of stages of
development for supervisors:

> When I first started at Thamesmead, I was aware of the need to establish
> the credibility of the Unit with other professionals and agencies in the
> community. I was very aware also of my need to be seen as a 'teacher' or
> 'student unit supervisor'. I had not previously supervised any social work
> students, though I had some limited experience as a secondary school
> teacher . . . I had also been a student on a social work course and had been
> supervised in practice placements . . . I certainly needed 'students' so that
> I could be the 'teacher'. I did a lot of 'teaching', and with the benefit of
> hindsight I think that *there was probably a lot more teaching than learning going on
> at that time.* Some of the students seem to learn a lot, but I regret that others
> apparently learn very little from me . . . (emphasis added)

This stage of development was characterized by a preoccupation with *teaching*.
It seemed to suit some students, to be coped with by others, but for a few it was
apparently not helpful at all. Later, I became interested in using the student
group as a vehicle for supervision:

> I experimented with joint supervision of the students in twos and threes,
> and with group supervision where about six to eight students might be
> involved. I discovered the hard way that whilst joint supervision, with a
> focus on the direct practice of students with their clients worked with small
> numbers of students, it did not work with more than about three, or
> occasionally four in the group . . .
>
> I began to see that students learned in very different ways, and that they
> used the supervision sessions differently. Some were open and readily
> talked about their feelings of uncertainty or delight, others were closed or
> private (at least to me) about their learning. During the same period, I
> came increasingly into contact with students and teachers from other
> professions, and began to come up against the expectations (which they
> brought from their own college-based experience) of *how* teaching and
> learning should go in the practice component of their training.
>
> I tried to distinguish characteristic patterns for medical students, for health
> visitor students, and for social work students – but at such a level of
> generality the categorizations were inappropriately broad, and imprecise.
> Instead I began to try to distinguish differences within the professional
> groupings of the students, as well as between them. I began, for example, to
> look for the differences between those social work students on post-
> graduate and those on non-graduate CQSW courses. This attempt was

equally unhelpful. I began to recognize that students had different ways of learning which were not directly due to their intended profession, nor to the academic level of course they were on . . .

This recognition that students learned in different ways occurred largely in parallel with the recognition that supervisors might have distinctive or different ways of teaching. I realized in meetings of groups of supervisors at colleges, and even more so at group meetings of student unit supervisors in the region, that we did not all teach in the same way. I began to realize that the way in which some supervisors related to their students was much more authoritarian whilst others seemed to be in less hierarchical relationships with their students.

I began to realize that I could help students whose approach might be different from how I was teaching – if I managed to abandon what I had thought of as the *right* way to supervise. The students' learning was not synonymous with my teaching. I also began to see that congruence between my approach and how the student learned was not the only kind of successful fit – as some marriages work on the basis of the complementarity so, apparently, could supervision.

A further step in this process was the recognition that not only were there differences between students, but that the same student might use different approaches at various stages in the same placement or for different learning tasks in the same time period.

All of these reflections confirmed the need for those who were specialist supervisors to develop a range of approaches, and to provide a range of teaching and diverse learning experiences for students. Similarly there was a need to provide formal and informal learning opportunities in the student group to make use of their combined experience.

Therefore, the learning contract at Thamesmead included the following (Gardiner/CCETSW 1978):

(v) an indication of the student's stage of professional development and his current learning needs for this placement need clarification, as does the student's usual style of learning. If a student can be helped before and during the placement to identify his own learning processes then he can play a full and active part in the learning/teaching.
(vi) the practice teacher's individual learning/teaching styles will need to be identified to either provide congruence with the student's learning styles, or to provide an opportunity to teach/learn in a different way . . .

Although the terms *style* and *stage* were used in this contract they were not defined, and at that time had been developed independently of the work on these concepts in the adult learning literature. The notion of *style* encompassed ideas like 'prefers to read first and try things out later', or 'usually gets some experience first and then tries to make sense of it'.

The term *stage* was related more to 'the development of professional identity as a social worker' on the one hand, and to 'a cycle of learning stages' on the other. These stages in the cycle included notions like 'being open to new learning', 'owning and internalizing that experience', 'making use of that learning in practice', 'consolidating and being quite closed to new learning' in not very precisely-defined ways.

A role play, and alternative approaches to supervision

This third autobiographical account is of a role play at a conference for experienced supervisors. Because contemporaneous notes were made by two of the participants, it is possible to describe it with some accuracy, together with some subsequent discussion. Supervisors took the roles of student, supervisor, and observer. The notes made by the latter two participants are reproduced here in an abbreviated form.

The role play was of a first supervision session for a student in a residential placement with mentally ill clients. There had been a problem in the first group meeting which the student had attended when she had shared a good deal of information about herself to overcome a long silence in the group. Other staff had been unhappy about this intervention.

The supervision session began with a good deal of questioning by the supervisor to elicit details of the incident, after which he asked the student about her reading in the area, and her understanding of group processes. Afterwards there was a discussion about how the student copes when she has problems, and about the timing of self-disclosure, especially with clients who have recently had considerable problems of their own, and lack emotional resources and support. The student agreed that these were important factors, and was beginning to acknowledge that there could be a different way of doing things.

The student acknowledged that although she had first claimed she had said things to make the clients feel comfortable, it was also intended to make her feel comfortable too.

The student said 'You are saying I'm wrong, what should I do?', and 'How can I face them again?'. The supervisor did not respond by giving answers directly but instead said he would respond by asking how the student learns best and come back to the questions in another way.

The student backtracked here and got fed up – saying that the supervisor hadn't dealt with her feelings. The supervisor said that if she were in role as a student she would not have said that. All three participants then came out of role and discussed the role play.

The supervisor said that he was consciously not dealing with the feelings of anxiety initially – and that although the student was getting annoyed at first, she was later able to begin to use what was being offered. The observer agreed with this. The supervisor said that he would have gone on by showing the student the connections between what she was trying to unload in the supervision (her feelings about being rejected by the group) and the pressure she felt to unload how she felt in the group session itself.

Both the student and the observer felt that they 'would have tried to deal with the anxiety feelings first'.

The supervisor (in the role play) wrote:

In the discussion I asked why I should deal with the anxiety first. There seemed to be four different answers given by the others:

1. to get it out of the way first
2. to be where the student was
3. it's what we are best at
4. to look at their feelings about themselves and then at the (social work) task

It seemed to me that the educational process of supervision was being described as 'emptying the bucket of anxiety which the student was carrying'. I felt that if I were to try to deal with the feelings of the student first then I would probably be colluding with the student . . . I would be allowing her to spill out all of her feelings when that was not the primary purpose of the supervision session. I felt from her account of the group that she was not very good at holding off her own needs and was rather greedy for attention to her own feelings. I felt that she was trying to run supervision in the same way and I was not prepared to let her do this . . .

I also said that I was reluctant to consider making students over-dependent since they were adults and I did not see it was my job to be 'their emotional nursemaid'.

Towards the end of the discussion I said that I thought that I had responded to, and acknowledged, the concerns of the student in other ways – by being interested in her experiences, by providing a structure and meaning for her experiences, and by acknowledging that we all have that kind of problem as beginning practitioners. In this way I felt that I was refusing to set myself up above her as an expert or paragon in opposition to her incompetence. I did not feel I have to verbalise acknowledging her anxiety nor focus the supervision on it. I had shown it in other ways.

There is some evidence here of at least two kinds of educational model. First is the traditional, almost stereotypical social casework model of supervision. The supervisor playing the student, and the observer, felt that they would deal with the student's feelings in the supervisory relationship, as they would with a client if they were the worker.

Second, there is an attempt to acknowledge and contain those feelings in the context of a more equal teaching/learning relationship which does not turn the student into a kind of client who must depend on the supervisor to handle difficult and uncomfortable feelings. This role play is a particularly useful example, because as often happens in practice placements, the student's problems in her practice are reflected in what she tries to do in supervision. Both these supervisors thought 'dealing with feelings' was a legitimate thing to do because 'it is what we are best at'. This means, of course, 'what we are best at' *as practitioners*, not necessarily as supervisors.

Clearly, there is a need to look at what demonstrably occurs in supervision sessions, and how students and supervisors try to make sense of the experiences. Such research would need to be descriptive and illuminative, as well as interpretative. The next section summarizes the research problem, and explicitly identifies what this study set out to accomplish. It then addresses the problems of designing such research, and the methodology need to produce such data.

2.5   The nature of the research problem and some methodological issues

The three autobiographical accounts in the previous section show that the influence of the classical literature has continued through to the 1980s. Therefore it is now possible to set out the components of the research problems which this study tries to address:

1. despite half of the total time spent on social work training courses being in supervised practice placements, *the practice component in general, and the supervisory process in particular, is under-researched;*
2. the *literature on the supervision process is dated, and derived from an American model of social casework supervision;*
3. *American-based social casework has been largely supplanted as a model of practice* in United Kingdom social work agencies, so an isomorphic model should not simply be casework-based;
4. the *language, concepts and terminology used to describe events in supervision, and give meaning to them, are illustrations of concept-leakage* from the practice arena to the teaching/learning arena;
5. the *literature generalizes* about *all* teachers, and *all* students;
6. the *literature reflects a traditional, hierarchical model of teaching and learning*, which values the knowledge of the teacher and the discipline, rather than the experience of the learner;
7. the *classical model establishes a hierarchy of hierarchies*, with clients and students at the bottom, agency supervisors in the middle, and college based tutors at the top;
8. the *literature sees teaching and learning problems as the outcome of individual learning pathologies*, often related to the anxiety of students about change and emotional growth, and does not take account of the interactive nature of the supervisory relationship;
9. the model *emphasises instruction as the teaching mode*, rather than the facilitation of student learning;
10. the *educational task is seen as the acquisition of knowledge by the student, from his teachers, and its application to 'real life' practice.*

Some of these components overlap others, and it is not an exhaustive list. However, it provides sufficient justification for the focus and purpose of this research, which is not simply an attempt to add to the detail of knowledge in an area of study. Instead, it faces the challenge of producing explanations which are meaningful to those being studied, and useful to others in social work education. To the extent to which it is successful in this intention, the study will have implications for the college-based tutor/student relationship, and more widely for the teaching and learning activities throughout social work education and training. The findings will also be relevant to other professional and vocational training – especially where they are rooted in models which are teacher- and discipline-centred.

Thus, in addressing these aspects of the research problem, some or all of the following must be produced:

1. *descriptions of the events in supervision derived from direct evidence* of actual supervision sessions and current placements, not second-hand, nor subsequent, reporting of past experiences at a level of generality which obscures what is happening in individual supervision sessions;
2. *accounts of the interpretations and meanings which those involved attach to their experiences,* in supervision sessions at the time, and subsequently;
3. *the recognition of patterns in those experiences, and the building of concepts and frameworks* which can account for these where existing explanations are inadequate or misleading;
4. *offering feedback, to those involved, of explanations and interpretations derived from the recognition of these patterns;*
5. *the development of generalizations from case illustrations* as the *basis of a new model of learning in social work education,* which could be useful to others in social work education and elsewhere;
6. *influence, directly and indirectly, on developments in social work education,* through the publication of findings at professional conferences and in the literature, and through contributions to the developing policies and practices of the validating body (CCETSW).

Such a range of aims for the research study was ambitious, and required the development of methods of enquiry to produce the required data. Such methods of data collection, to allow the identification of individual experiences, and the generation of new meanings and new interpretations, are not currently widely used in social work education. However, they are necessary to find out, in social work supervision, 'how anybody at all learns how to distinguish the true from the generally accepted' (Ryan 1987). The close inter-personal nature of social work and supervision suggests that methods used and developed to study them must be sensitive to the subtleties of interactions within individual supervision sessions, and for placements as a whole. Therefore the educational evaluation literature was explored to find how others had addressed the problems of collecting these kinds of qualitative data, including the sense participants made of their experiences.

Traditionally, scientific research has an objective, detached observer who records data which are later scrutinized for patterns, and related to what is already known in the field. Such an approach is not easily applied to complex processes with many variables in 'real-life' rather than laboratory settings. Until relatively recently, educational research involved testing hypotheses about parts of the learning process, but was justifiably criticized for only measuring what was quantifiable. Much of what would be needed to explore the interactions between individual teachers and learners (as in social work supervision) will need to be studied where it arises – in placements.

In looking at the supervisory process, the present author has some advantages over the conventionally detached observer – he has been a student and a specialist supervisor in the roles to be researched. Whilst those experiences allow an informed, insider's understanding of the culture of supervision, it also has the potential for misperceptions and preconceptions to be compounded or to remain unchecked. The study was therefore designed and developed in ways which could maximize the value of being a kind of insider, but which would also ensure that possible bias and evaluator-effects could be directly addressed with the subjects of the study, and with others in social work education.

Similar problems are described in the literature where educational evaluators have undertaken research into their own institution, course or department (Adelman and Alexander 1983). Similarly, experiences of the educational evaluator being part of the project which he has been evaluating have been described (Jaques 1982), and the problems which may arise when the role of the evaluator was unclear, or different from the expectations of those who were being evaluated, have also been reported (Gardiner 1984c).

The political and other contexts of the evaluation are critical, since one can legitimately ask 'Who is the evaluation for?' In the present study, the answer is multiple: for the teachers and students being studied, for others in social work education, for the evaluator, and so on, because 'No evaluation is neutral' (Macdonald and Walker 1977). It was made clear to all who took part that this research was not being undertaken by CCETSW, but was personal research by an individual researcher.

Since Parlett and Hamilton's paper on illuminative approaches (1971), considerable attention has been given to the style and methodology of educational evaluation. Attempts have been made to match the evaluative approach to the subject of the study. In particular, much has been made of the limitations of traditional quantitative approaches. The strength of the traditional approach to educational evaluation is the claim to reflect what is thought to be scientific and rational. It therefore is presumed to have credibility and status with those who do not know intimately what has been evaluated, but who know and value the scientific paradigm as a medium of investigation.

This scientific paradigm, described also as the agricultural-botany paradigm by Parlett and Hamilton, is essentially concerned with problems of cause and effect. However, proponents of the newer illuminative paradigms would argue that what is needed is to address issues of meaning, in a descriptive and interpretative study of the nature of teaching and learning.

This kind of naturalistic enquiry has two advantages: it allows whole areas of educational activity to be studied, not partial, quantifiable elements; and teachers and learners can be studied in their ordinary, everyday experiences of teaching and learning.

None of this, of course, is unique to educational evaluation. In other disciplines, including the natural sciences, similar developments have also been made to move away from the simple models of explanation of *cause and effect* to those of *meaning*; and away from those looking at *events* to those which look at *process* i.e. 'relations' (Elton and Laurillard 1979). The social sciences have persisted in using a traditional scientific paradigm to frame research long after those within the natural science disciplines had recognized its limitations; and long after it had been accepted there that the notion of a detached objective observer was an unrealistic aim even in the kinds of research which involves inanimate objects (Russell 1910):

> The traditional conception of cause and effect is one which modern science shows to be quite fundamentally erroneous, and requiring to be replaced by a quite different notion, that of laws of change.

Furthermore, natural scientists have realized for more than half a century now that the *things* and *events* which they study are not simply *objects* at all. This followed the discovery after two thousand years that the atom (previously believed to be the smallest unit of matter in the universe) was not only divisible and composed of smaller particles, but at its core was a series of complex processes. This, of course, has profound implications for those who seek to utilize the classical scientific methods of enquiry into the relationships between objects, since there is a need to develop the language and concepts of *process* rather than those of *events*, and of *transactions* rather than *things*.

There are other parallels outside the natural sciences. In many other academic disciplines there is evidence of the abandonment of the traditional scientific paradigm. To take one example, in psychotherapy, the importance of a focus on interaction and process is recognized as part of a search for interpretation and meaning rather than simply cause and effect. We may recognize these paradigm shifts as indications of the maturity of a discipline which can give up the borrowed respectability and status derived from traditional scientific models, and begin to develop theory which is grounded in the processes observed and described within its field of study.

Rycroft (1966) has shown the way in which psychoanalysts sought to defend the scientific base of their discipline against criticisms from Eysenck (1965) and others by stressing its value as a causal theory. However, Rycroft recognizes that both parties in this argument make the mistake of

> assuming that it is only the physical sciences which are intellectually respectable. It is perhaps relevant here that ... both psychology and medicine are faculties which suffer from an inferiority complex in relation to science.

Rycroft also recognizes the implications here of Szasz's attack on the very concept of mental illness itself being a kind of myth (1962), and that psychoanalysis is not a causal theory, but a semantic one. Rycroft continues:

> What Freud did here was not to explain the patient's choice causally but to understand it and give it meaning, and the procedure he was engaged in was not the scientific one of elucidating causes, but the semantic one of making sense of it. It can be argued here that much of Freud's work was really semantic and that he made a revolutionary discovery in semantics . . . that neurotic symptoms are meaningful disguised communications, but that, owing to his scientific training and allegiance, he formulated his findings in the conceptual framework of the physical sciences.

This distinction between cause and meaning is a helpful one for present purposes because it identifies the limitations of the scientific model of cause and effect in accounting for the content *and* process of the interactions between two people. There are parallel lessons in thinking about the methodology to be employed in a study of meaning rather than of cause, and Rycroft again identifies an important corollary:

> If psycho-analysis is recognised as a semantic theory, not a causal one, its theory can start where its practice does – in the consulting room . . .

By formulating what he was doing in terms which gave scientific credibility, and which were derived from his own experience as a physical scientist, Freud could be said to have obscured what was actually going on in his consulting room. Perhaps this is an earlier example of the problems which follow from concept-leakage – in this case from the natural sciences to the psychoanalytic consulting room.

One must be wary in general of such dangers in educational evaluation, and in this present kind of study in particular. Rycroft and Szasz both extend the analysis into the roots of the psychoanalytic model and terminology. The lesson to be learnt is that any study of meaning in supervision in social work education must focus upon the equivalent of the consulting room – the supervision session itself and the meanings the participants ascribe to events in it. In that way, it would be possible to study the teaching and learning processes of supervision in their own natural context – and it is as well to remember that all behaviour taken out of the context in which it arises can become meaningless.

2.6   Quantitative and qualitative educational evaluation

Lawton (1980) provides an overview which helps to identify the key dimensions of educational evaluation, both in terms of data collection and the presentation of results. He offers six models. The first is a traditional experimental type, with before and after measures to test the impact of some intervening treatment – rather like the effect of a new fertilizer on plant growth. He draws attention to the limitations of the approach, including the fact that human beings tend to act differently when observed, and that they respond in individual ways which may not be susceptible to large-scale, averaged results. Educational programmes may have long timescales in both implementation and effect, which makes the isolation of independent variables very difficult.

Lawton calls his second model an industrial factory model, which is concerned with improving or testing a product. Typically, the evaluator will be trying to translate broad aims into measurable, specific objectives, and to devise and administer tests to measure the effects. There are obvious limitations to this model, which include the specifying of objectives in behavioural terms, the problems of representative samples, together with the exclusion of potentially useful formative material. There is also a more general criticism of this model: that the context of the educational institution itself is excluded from the focus of the evaluation.

Objections to these first two models lead to other perspectives, which can contribute more directly to the areas excluded from traditional evaluations and, particularly, to respond to the problems of sample size needed to produce statistically valid outcomes. The third model is derived from Parlett and Hamilton's work on illuminative evaluation (1971).

An important factor here, which bears attention in the present study, is the question of the state of knowledge in a particular subject area, and the need to map out broad areas descriptively first, even when more detailed or quantifiable work might usefully follow. The illuminative approach is not without its difficulties, and its critics. Particular attention has been drawn to the problems of collecting such data, and the skills required. There has been debate about the extent to which evaluators are participants or observers in the events they describe, and their relation to those they are engaged with both in the programme, and those who have set up the evaluation (Gardiner and Mathias 1988). There have also been debates about the skills required for such work. We have, elsewhere (Gardiner 1984c) described the difficulties in an educational evaluation project where the involvement of an external evaluator skewed the inter-professional training programme in the community:

> (The evaluation project) . . . did *not* observe, describe, record and offer interpretations of inter-professional work and learning, which is my understanding of what such evaluation is about. It did *not* look at examples of joint practice that naturally arose, nor did it observe or record supervision sessions based on such practice. In short, it only gathered up data from sessions which the evaluation project itself set up.
>
> I believe that what the Thamesmead Project did was to evaluate and focus on *its own impact* on inter-professional work and learning in the community, rather like a pebble measuring ripples in a pond only after it had been thrown in . . .

These are important warnings for those of us who take on such roles, and there is clearly a need for such workers to be skilled interviewers, observers, and to have some knowledge and understanding of the culture and assumptions of those who are being researched if we are to study students and supervisors in natural settings. It is in this connection that the personal experiences reported earlier should be seen, since they served two main purposes. They provided data which allowed the articulation of a research problem; and they gave direct evidence of the biases and preconceptions of the researcher, derived from his previous experiences in similar situations to those now being studied. This responds to those who call for the value position and possible biases of a researcher always to be made explicit (Mann 1987).

Mann has articulated a number of areas where researchers 'should know ourselves' in this kind of study:

1. What do I – the researcher – bring to the research situation in terms of knowledge and past experiences, attitudes, values and beliefs?
2. How do these personal contributions affect how I find out something and what I find out?
3. What can this tell me about how I – and others – learn?
4. What views do I implicitly express through my research approach about the people I am researching and about how they learn?
5. Is this a view I want to express . . .
6. What views are expressed by the theory and research in which I ground my work?

Lawton's fourth model is a political one, based largely on the work of Macdonald (1976) who identified three ideal-types of evaluations. Objective, value-free evaluation is not possible because all evaluations take place in a real political context. Thus his bureaucratic, autocratic and democratic types reflect their relation to funders and decision-makers. Of most relevance here is the democratic one, where the data collected must be reported in ways which are accessible to non-specialists, so that they are enabled to make judgements in the area under study. Whilst his formulation is an ideal-type, these elements of the present research have been explicitly acknowledged earlier. This echoes Stake's notion (1977) that evaluations should be 'responsive' and take account of multiple audiences for the work, including those who have been researched, as well as the academic community, and funding bodies.

The fifth model which Lawton identifies is the practitioner-researcher model. In general terms, this is about research-based practice, or practice-based research. Lawton suggests that this changes the emphasis from independent evaluation to self-evaluation, and the parallels with action-research modes in many of the social sciences are clear.

The sixth eclectic, or case study, model brings together case study approaches (to the collection, and/or presentation of data) and multiple method approaches. It would seem that there are possibly two models interwoven here – one which sees case studies as an opportunity for holistic evaluations and interpretations, and the other which brings together multiple methodologies.

There is some limited evidence of qualitative evaluation methods being used in social work education. Earlier, reference was made to the CCETSW study of practice placements (Syson and Baginsky 1981) which collected data by interview methods from forty-one CQSW placements in some depth, paying particular attention to arrangements for setting them up, and the expectations of students, supervisors and tutors. They saw the possible alternatives as either a broad, impressionistic study, or a narrower one using 'representative samples and statistical techniques'. However, there are other ways of identifying research problems, including using the study to describe, illumine and clarify some of the key issues at stake, and to allow both the focus and methods of the study to develop in the light of the findings at each stage.

Miller (1983) has provided a guide to such evaluation research methods for those in social work, in which she describes a methodological approach with the following criteria (which reflect the pattern adopted in this study):

- it is practitioner-oriented, that is, its chief function is to provide information and insight for professional educators and students;
- it is problem centred, with 'problems' defined as issues and concerns arising from the particular teaching and learning setting being studied;
- it has flexible methodology, which is not fully pre-specified by the researcher in advance, but is responsive to the situation as it is studied, and open to different methods in different contexts;
- it is cross-disciplinary, being open to drawing on methods and concepts developed in different disciplines – not just in psychology for example, but also social anthropology (e.g. for approaches to field work research), sociology (e.g. participant observation), history (e.g. document analysis and interpretation);
- it is heuristically organised, that is, the research issues are progressively redefined as the study goes on and new data emerges.

Despite Miller's paper, there is very little evidence in the social work literature of the penetration of these ideas. Indeed, as Sheldon (1986) illustrates, there is still a strong swing of the pendulum towards more scientific and outcome-oriented studies, which could make social work more respectable as an academic discipline. It might be suspected here that some of the problems which social work teachers have in this respect come from their lack of academic background and research experience. Dinerman (1983) has looked from the perspective of American social work education at the faculty (i.e. the staff) of British social work courses, and found that almost forty per cent of the college-based staff (including those who teach on degree and post-graduate courses) did not themselves have a first degree. Against that background, the attempt to establish credibility through following the well-trodden path of the scientific method perhaps becomes more understandable.

Patton (1980) has described the kinds of situations in which qualitative evaluation approaches are appropriate. He includes:

1. where the focus is on *educational process*;
2. where there are *individualised or widely diverse outcomes*;
3. where the *intention is to be formative for the recipients of the evaluation*;
4. where *unobtrusive methods* are necessary;

5. where the *quality of outcomes is more important than quantity*.

Whilst any one of these conditions might suggest the use of qualitative methods of enquiry, in fact each of these conditions is relevant to the present study. Using personalized methods in a field such as social work is important, since the practice of social work is about skilled, sensitive, inter-personal transactions. Thus, research methods must seem (to those being studied) able to take account of, but not distort, the nuances and subtleties of both social work and the supervision process.

Even if more quantitative research were desirable, the stage which has been reached in the study of supervision is not sufficient for specification of the dimensions and categories along which more quantifiable research could be pursued. Therefore the state of the art also points to using qualitative methods.

The process of interviewing as a means of data collection, hypothesis building and testing out with those from whom the data have been collected, leading to refining and reformulating hypotheses, is the essential basis of working with families in social work practice. This form of evaluation is congruent and consonant with the experience of social workers in general and the researcher in particular. Feedback following data collection suggested that, for those involved, the methods employed encouraged them to be open and free in their responses.

Similarly, a focus on the interactive process and on the impact of the worker on a situation, together with monitoring the impact of the situation on the worker, is commonplace in both social work and qualitative evaluation.

Since this study is also intended to begin the process of generating models grounded in the experience of supervision itself, data must be collected and then interpreted in ways which can contribute to that process. Glaser and Strauss (1967) make this clear:

> The continual intermeshing of data collection and analysis has direct bearing on how the research is brought to a close. When the researcher is convinced that his conceptual framework forms a systematic theory, that it is a reasonably accurate statement of the matter studied, that it is couched in a form which is possible for others to use in studying a similar area, and that he can publish the results with confidence, then he has neared the end of his research . . . Why does the researcher trust what he knows? . . . They are *his* perceptions, *his* personal experiences, *his* hard won analyses. A field worker knows that he knows, not only because he has been in the field . . . and seen how our intervention can be used for good or ill, and because he has discovered and carefully generated hypotheses, but also because 'in his bones' he feels the worth of his final analysis. He has been living with the partial analyses for many months, testing them each step of the way, until he has built his theory.

There are a few general methodological points which relate to the entire study – the confidentiality of all material was offered and agreed, so that no individual could be identified. Sometimes this has meant slightly disguising locations, or other identifying features, in the reporting of data. Questions like how to negotiate entry and how to enter situations were considered. The pattern in most cases has been to use known individuals to negotiate entry for interviews with those unknown. This was true in two senses – one was with supervisors initiating contact with their students; the other was in supervisors setting up contact with their colleagues.

A further general question relates to how the focus and purpose of the research was presented, both in establishing contact, and in introductions. This was always done by saying that the research was about *how teaching and learning took place in supervision*, as opposed to simply *what was learnt*, or *how well* it had been learnt. The researcher also introduced himself as someone who had trained as a social worker, and who had supervised a large number of students. In a small number of cases, it was mentioned that in the role of student unit supervisor, the researcher himself had also been on the receiving end of evaluative research (Kings Fund 1986; Jaques 1982) and that had not always been very easy (Gardiner 1984c). This echoes a concern of Patton (1980):

> Evaluation is too serious a matter to be done by someone who has never been a client in a program.

Patton also cautions about sampling strategies and the need to consider whether to distinguish between random, stratified random and cluster samples, and the dangers inherent in studying extreme or deviant examples if we expect to be able to generalize the findings to other situations. Therefore, in collecting new data, situations where the results would be dismissed because the source is recognizably special, deviant, or extreme were avoided.

There are two initial needs in data collection: to gather data directly from supervisors, to look at their current ideas about how they supervise, and why they do it in this way; and to gather data about what actually goes on in supervision sessions, to report them without re-interpretation, and then to look at the issues raised. These focal areas are not of the same order, and are therefore likely to require different methods even though both are intended to generate qualitative rather than quantitative data.

It was decided to use the opportunity presented by a national conference of a supervisors' organization to ask all of those attending (usually 30 to 40) to complete questionnaires designed to elicit this kind of material. At the same time, and to complement this breadth of focus, a 'not untypical' supervisor from amongst them was asked whether she would tape-record all of the supervision sessions in a forthcoming placement, and make these available week by week to the researcher.

Later in the study sampling strategies were devised to encompass wide variation across certain ranges. For example, the geographical distribution of placements studied covered Northern Ireland, the north of Scotland, English urban, rural, and metropolitan areas; placements from both graduate and non-graduate courses were studied, and some attempt was made to include smaller and larger courses. Two pairs of interviews about CSS placements were added during the study, to take account of the policy developments towards a single new social work qualification.

The final general point about methodology considered here concerns time sampling. The story of the explorer who sought the magical taste of a rare fruit but was disappointed at the taste of the flower is a useful reminder that what is observed will vary according to the time of the observation, and that unless time factors are taken into account it can be easy to mistake the meaning of what is found. In the initial data collection phase, an entire placement was studied, even though this was relatively costly in terms of time and resources. In the questionnaire exercise, information was asked for about all students, as well as particular individual students or placements.

Qualitative approaches can have advantages in a study like this one, but some concerns remain, especially about how to validate data which consist of both observations and interpretations. There are two main ways in which this can be achieved. First is to check out with those from whom the data are collected that they are accurate, and that any selection of material, interpretations, and presentation of material confirms or adds to their understanding and experience of what is described. These checks, including feedback to those who participated in the study, are described as they occur during the study.

A second way is to ensure multiple perspectives are brought to bear on experiences and meanings attributed to them. Thus a variety of methods and targets for data collection are used. This kind of approach is often called 'triangulation' because whilst each method might give relatively imprecise findings (like a ship's distress signal picked up by one coastal station), a more precise position can be plotted from several stations than from a single one, even if the latter were a stronger signal.

Thus, in the first stage of data collection, we shall employ a broad beam covering a group of experienced supervisors, to look at how they say they teach and learn; and a more focused spotlight to illumine the subtle interactions in supervision sessions throughout a placement.

The collection of data is intended to be sufficiently holistic to allow the presentation of data to be in a form which enables whole cases to be considered. This is especially important in the generation of grounded models, because the specific contexts in which the data were collected can also be considered. Accordingly, later case examples bring together data collected at different points in the study, and by different methods.

3

Initial Data Collection

3.1   A questionnaire for supervisors

The earlier autobiographical reports suggested that it was important to collect data about how supervisors expected to teach, and how they expected their students to learn. This questionnaire exercise was intended to generate descriptions of how supervisors had themselves learnt, in what they considered to have been an important learning experience. Equally, it was hoped to produce descriptions of how supervisors preferred to teach. It was also intended to explore whether there might be links between how the supervisors had learned, in this significant experience, and how they taught or expected their students to learn.

Thirty-nine supervisors who were attending a national conference were asked to complete two sheets. They were told that the primary aim in completing the first sheet was to help identify teaching and learning styles, and possible links between them. The second sheet was to look at the impact of teaching and learning styles in supervision.

They were told that the researcher would treat all material in the responses as confidential, and that no individuals would be identified in any subsequent report. The questions on this first sheet were deliberately unspecific so that any kind of learning experience could be described. As a result a range of content areas were covered but there were some similarities in the learning processes described. What this exercise would NOT show, of course, is whether the learning styles or strategies reported are characteristic ones for these individuals. Laurillard (1978) has shown that it would be surprising if this were the case, since her study points to the discriminating way adult learners adapt their learning to meet the requirements of the particular learning context. She says:

> It was possible to show that certain types of cognitive descriptors, namely forms of differences in learning style, were indeed applicable to the data collected, but not in the expected way. It was not possible to demonstrate that students exhibited consistent differences in their approach to a task, but it was possible to show that the differences were applicable to a student

in a particular learning context. Thus the same students could exhibit different characteristics on different occasions.

What the data here demonstrate are the strategies which were actually used by the supervisors in what they described as significant learning experiences for them. Whilst the response may be only one strategy within a repertoire of strategies for some people, for others it may be their only (or at least their usual) approach.

Sheet One was completed and returned by thirty-four people. It was collected before Sheet Two was administered, and it asked respondents to:

1. Describe briefly an important learning experience for them
2. Describe WHAT they had learnt from this experience
3. Describe HOW they had learnt from this experience

The responses which were returned reported experiences as diverse as how the family in which one grew up affected one's personal development, and how someone had learnt to ride a bicycle as a child. These experiences fell into four main categories of learning: personal development (6 people), professional practice (7), being a learner (9), and being a teacher (12).

There were some common elements in the descriptions of how learning had occurred, including:

1. the importance of a challenge and/or pain in the experience, and the motivation to overcome it;
2. the importance of the reflective process after an important experience to make sense of it – sometimes alone and often with the help of a significant other person to help in that process;
3. the importance of a framework in which to locate experiences and make them meaningful.

Some people did not return this first sheet. Discussion subsequently with two of these supervisors suggested that they had used the opportunity to describe particularly painful personal experiences which they had found helpful to explore, but they did not wish to hand in the completed forms. One of these had described the recent loss of a close relative. It is not unreasonable to assume that the responses in the unreturned sheets were not markedly different – although it seems likely that those who described events related to personal growth and development are consequently under-represented. Certainly there are differences of approach to learning reported by these supervisors, which were not obviously related to the content of the significant learning they had described.

Sheet Two was also returned by thirty-four people. It asked respondents to:

1. Describe briefly HOW they preferred to teach
2. Describe a student they had found difficult to supervise
3. Say why it had been difficult to supervise this student

4. Suggest how the student could have been better supervised (either by themselves or someone else).

The responses in general appear to represent a statement of value position for this relatively experienced group of supervisors. Most said that they preferred to supervise in a way which valued the experience of the student, and which was not a reflection of traditional hierarchical relationships between teachers and learners. However, these were not always the terms used by the respondents themselves. Typical of the responses to question one (about HOW they preferred to teach) on this second sheet is:

Informal sessions where we both can feel relaxed. Start off from what the student has done/been involved in, and draw issues from that so it is based on discussion, exchange of ideas, experiences, etc., but I suppose I do a lot of the leading into the areas to be covered.

There were some respondents who recognized the need for structures to work within, as well as having a mutually interactive relationship with the student:

Sharing obligations, experience, and expectations openly in an initial contract and subsequent sub-contracts.

Within an agreed framework but with enough flexibility for either to add or subtract – it can be directive or non-directive for either if necessary.

The students with whom these supervisors had difficulty were those who 'needed direct teaching', 'lacked confidence', 'wanted theoretical knowledge', 'wanted me to be an expert' and most of all those who 'split intellectual and feeling experience and denied failure'. The supervisors reported that these students made them feel 'frustrated', 'angry and unsure', and 'vulnerable'. It is notable (again) that the language could also be used to describe interactions between workers and clients.

In describing such problems, some supervisors appeared to be teaching in a way which was not entirely consistent with their preferred position (of valuing the experience of the student), and seemingly they had some difficulty in teaching students who were unable, or unwilling, to take some responsibility for their own learning. Typically, these supervisors (as in the classical literature) tended to deal with the situation by seeing a student they found difficult to supervise as having individual learning pathologies, and they attributed responsibility to the student for a mis-match of conceptions or expectations:

she was dull, unmotivated and difficult to engage

his ideas do not merit his selection as a student . . . he is not keen to learn and unwilling to try things

(needing) everything spelled out . . . with a need for certainty and security

quiet, uncertain students who need a lot of babying.

Whilst the questionnaire allowed the gathering of the preliminary data from a group of supervisors, the exercise did not allow the immediate follow up of the responses. This suggested that subsequent phases of the study should include interviewing sessions, and that the sample might include following up some of these respondents.

In the replies, there was often a tension between what supervisors preferred, or expected, and what they were actually trying to do with some of the students. This tends to suggest that many of these supervisors were not versatile in their approaches to teaching, and did not readily discriminate between students' different approaches to learning in supervision.

This is an important finding, because it shows that supervisors in this group were able to describe the ways they preferred to teach, and could recognize that for some students there was a mis-match between this approach and how the student expected to learn, but they were unable (or chose not) to vary their preferred teaching approach to respond to these differences. Indeed, some explicitly thought that it would need to be a different supervisor e.g. a 'more directive', or 'less demanding' supervisor, to deal with those students.

Sometimes there were connections between responses to the two sheets – one participant explicitly linked learning to ride a bicycle with a student who needed direct teaching. Another respondent was less able to make these connections explicit:

> I learned that it was permissible – and what a relief – to say I don't really do this job very well (Sheet One)

> He is unwilling to try things – to make mistakes – and to experiment or consider changing (Sheet Two)

There may be a link here between being able to take risks, and being able to acknowledge failure in oneself, and the difficulties (for this supervisor) in supporting a student to risk failure. This supervisor was followed up in the interview part of the study, and he also completed a learning styles exercise. The findings in each of these various elements of the study reinforced this interpretation, and the connection was accepted later by the supervisor himself (in an interview in the next phase of the study).

Reflections on the questionnaire exercise

This questionnaire exercise suggests that some supervisors seem to be relatively fixed in their teaching approaches. Despite wanting to value the experience of the learner and 'start from where the learner was' this did not always extend to changing approaches to their teaching. They seemed, in fact, to be starting where the teachers were, in their approach to teaching. Amongst those experienced supervisors in the group (especially the unit supervisors), there was considerable variation in the confidence with which they approached 'difficult' students.

Further analysis showed that regardless of the number of students supervised, and the length of time they had been supervising, there were other factors which affected how the supervisory process was seen, and consequently what happened in supervision. Certainly, there was evidence that teachers preferred to teach in ways which were essentially similar to the ways they had reported for their own significant learning, and they had difficulties with students who did not learn in that way. These difficulties had not been overcome simply by more supervisory experience, so some attention is given later in the study to supervisors' stages of development as teachers. The responses of those known to be relatively inexperienced as supervisors show some of them less thrown by difficult students than some of their more experienced colleagues. To test this out further, the next stage of data collection included supervisors undertaking the role for the first time as well as more experienced, specialist supervisors.

To summarize, then, the evidence in the questionnaire responses seems to indicate that some teachers seem to believe that there is only one right way to teach (the way they themselves learn, or were taught). Some have recognized that there might be other ways of supervising, but felt that students who learned differently would need to be supervised by someone else. A smaller group saw that the supervisor might need to use other approaches to teaching than the preferred one. These differences in conceptions of teaching and learning in supervision recur in all the data reported in this study.

However, this group of supervisors is not necessarily typical – they were self-selected by choosing to attend a conference, and were probably better motivated to develop their supervisory skills than some others. They also included a larger proportion of specialist supervisors – student unit supervisors – than might be the case in a random group. However, the purpose of this part of the study was not to look for characteristics which would necessarily be applicable and generalizable to all supervisors. Instead, it was intended to see how some supervisors actually learnt and taught, and the kinds of problems they saw themselves as having. In this way, subsequent stages of the study could pay more attention to some of these specific issues, both with supervisors drawn from this group and elsewhere.

Continuing reflection suggested that there might be stages which learners go through, so the questions of match and mismatch (of supervisors and students) might need to be considered not only along a teaching/learning *style* dimension but one which was also related to *stages* of development. It was decided that this also should be explored more specifically in the later phase of data collection, and that any relevant literature on learning styles and developmental stages through which adult learners pass should be studied. The exploration of that literature is reported in Chapter Four.

3.2   A single case study

Whilst in the last section the broadly-focused questionnaire generated useful data about how supervisors view and describe their teaching and learning, it did not provide data about what they demonstrably do. This was especially important given the apparent gap between how supervisors said they preferred to teach, and problems they had with some students.

This single case study of the supervision sessions over an entire practice placement provides evidence of the kinds of transactions which demonstrably take place between a supervisor and student. It raises questions and issues which reflect back on the earlier data and, in turn, contribute to the selection and focus for the material collected and methodology in the rest of the study.

This exercise involved a supervisor and student agreeing to tape-record their supervision sessions during a four month placement and to make the tapes available to the researcher on a weekly basis. In the original arrangement, negotiated with the supervisor, it was agreed that it would be inappropriate for the researcher to comment at any stage on aspects of the student's performance either in his practice with his clients, or his performance in supervision. The supervisor negotiated the agreement with the student, who raised no objections to making tapes, and sending them to the researcher. It was agreed that the tapes were to be confidential to the researcher, and any reported material based on them would not include any identifying references to the supervisor or student.

Any comments made during the placement would be made only to the supervisor and would be related to helping her to identify her own style of teaching. Such comments were not intended to be evaluative of the quality of her teaching. There were no meetings planned to give this feedback in a systematic or formal way – instead there were occasional meetings with the supervisor in our usual work roles and a few telephone calls (prompted usually by the non-arrival of tapes for a couple of weeks).

It was felt, initially, that further contact might be a 'contaminant' which could affect the nature of the materials gathered. The setting up of the agreement pre-dated undertaking a full review of the literature on evaluative research. Subsequently, the supervisor was interviewed about the experience of tape-recording the sessions, even though this had not been intended at the beginning of the placement. In illuminative research such a contribution could be not only a legitimate part of the approach but could also have contributed to the validation of the findings.

The only direct contact with the student was at an informal lunch meeting at the end of the placement, when discussion included some feedback comments on his approach to learning during this placement, and on the teaching and learning which took place in the supervision sessions. At this point in the study, the emphasis was on looking at what supervisors do, and how they made sense of what went on in supervision sessions, to develop the work based on the questionnaire exercise.

As a direct result of the findings of this case study, there was greater concern to include material about students, and to focus attention on the interactions between teachers and students. The reasons for this shift of emphasis emerge in the commentaries on the supervision sessions.

The placement studied was the first placement on a two year non-graduate CQSW course. It lasted about sixteen weeks, for two days each week, with a small number of weeks in block placement. Supervision sessions were weekly, lasting one and a half to two hours. Tapes were to be made of each of them, though only twelve tapes were actually made. One of these was of poor sound quality and is not reported here. This placement was selected because it is not untypical, and avoids extreme or unusual features (Patton 1978). It took place in a statutory social services department.

The method adopted was chosen because it was relatively non-intrusive (i.e. there was not the distraction of an observer intruding into a two-person discussion) and yet gave fuller data than notes made by the participants or subsequent interviews where they could be asked for their recollections of what had gone on. However, there was some indication that both supervisor and student found that they were aware of being taped in the early part of the first few tapes, but they were less inhibited by it later in those sessions, and later in the placement as a whole.

The tape recordings were dealt with by playing them soon after they arrived, and making quite extensive notes during the first hearing. Key points, and particularly apposite quotations, were highlighted. The volume of material, together with the cost and time of doing so, militated against transcribing them in full. They are edited here to indicate salient features. The earlier supervision sessions are considered in more detail, to establish major themes and issues. The later sessions are dealt with more selectively, to highlight issues related to style and stage in teaching and learning, and to show the impact of assessment on the pattern of supervisory interaction.

The initial response to this material was to wonder at the richness and the depth of material collected, to remember students supervised in the Thamesmead Unit, and my own student experiences. Some sessions which seemed to struggle with issues I had met before (many times over) were particularly evocative. However there was much that was new and particular to this supervisor and student, and to the cases they were working with. It is the balance of the common and unique elements which this account seeks to reflect.

Listening to the tapes (especially on first hearing), sometimes prompted muttering or talking to the tape-recorder. Tape-recording is therefore better than direct observation for reasons which go beyond the detail of the record, because it allows the researcher to react openly to the interactions without distracting the participants.

The supervisor for this placement was female, and in her late thirties. She had been qualified for more than ten years before the placement began, and had previously supervised a small number of students, including some from the course which this student was undertaking. She had a role as a specialist practitioner in a social services department area office, in a metropolitan area. There was another student placed in the office, with a different supervisor, over the same period.

The student was male, in his early thirties. He had previously worked in residential social work, and as an unqualified social worker for some years in a social services area team in a nearby authority. A contract for the placement was agreed between student and supervisor. It describes the work the student is expected to undertake and the commitments he should make, but indicates rather fewer of the obligations of the supervisor.

The key issues examined in the data were the qualitative features of the teaching and learning interaction:

1. *the language used* by supervisor and student, and the extent to which it reflects social casework practice
2. *the concepts each appears to have of the teaching and learning processes*, and the impact these conceptions have on the expectations they bring to the supervisory relationship, including the extent of 'fit' of these conceptions
3. the *extent of hierarchy and directiveness in the supervisory relationship*
4. any *changes in the patterns of interaction* in supervision
5. the *impact of assessment on teaching and learning processes*

The material is presented in three sections as follows: Session One, Sessions Three to Five, and Session Six Onwards. Each section discusses the findings, then they are considered together in an overview of the chapter.

3.2.1 Single case study – session one

More attention is given to what took place in the first session because it sets the scene for the placement. Inevitably, with a large amount of data collected, this account is selective, to demonstrate the patterns of teaching and learning interaction in supervision.

In *Session One* the supervisor tries to establish a pattern and ground rules for the placement. She is apparently clear about how she will teach, and how the student should work with his clients. The session includes substantial discussions about the area team in which the placement occurs, and about an essay which the student has to write.

There was a lengthy introduction from the supervisor, who spoke a great deal, with very brief responses from the student. The first exchanges were rather awkward discussions about timings, and making arrangements for future sessions.

The supervisor asked the student whether he had 'anything to bring to the session'. The student said that he did not, and the discussion moved to the cases which the student was about to take on.

In the first case discussion the supervisor said 'I don't think there will be anything to sort out . . . it's probably a question of making arrangements to meet people . . . and I suggest making an appointment to see the school counsellor . . .'

The supervisor that said she 'wanted to get the admin bits out of the way first'. The student replied 'mmm . . .' doubtfully. The supervisor said 'There isn't anything else is there?' in a tone of voice which suggested that she was expecting the answer 'No'. The student said 'No.'

When the student began to describe the first case passed to him he was very formal and rather stilted in his use of language. He did not seem at ease.

The discussion turned to the team meeting earlier that day where there had been a case presented by one of the members for discussion. The supervisor said 'What did you think of the case discussion this morning?' The student said 'There are so many unknowns, aren't there . . . ?' and paused. The supervisor immediately said '(He) was picking up on . . .' and explained the situation. The student was silent . . .

The student introduced the idea of tape-recording his interviews. He felt that other kinds of reporting were not very satisfactory, and was concerned about how the supervisor would know if there were any problems. He went on to say 'I'm not used to all this writing' and then resisted the suggestion that if he taped his interviews he should make written comments for the supervisor as well.

The supervisor turned the focus again to the discussion in the team meeting. 'What did you think was going on . . . ?' The student said he felt 'an outsider'. The student used the word 'introspective' three times when talking about how he saw this team, and said this was 'very different' from his previous team, which was 'not so preoccupied with talking about their own experiences and feelings'. The supervisor went on at some length about 'struggles for power in the team'. The student thought 'all this was at a deep level' and did not respond when the supervisor continued to talk about 'the problems we have as a team'. The student openly said 'I'm not very interested in that kind of discussion'.

When pressed, the student made some comments about the 'studious approach in this team', and twice described them as 'serious'. He made a link with his earlier experience – the previous team in which he had worked 'made fun of themselves', and there was 'socializing in the office'. He observed that 'there is not a lot of laughter here'. The supervisor jumped in rather quickly to say that there had been an example of laughter in the meeting, but the student dismissed it as 'manic humour' and 'just a release'. The student took responsibility for terminating this part of the session by saying 'it has gone as far as is useful'.

The next part of the session was a discussion of an essay about interviewing. The student said that 'one could choose one's own title'. The supervisor made some uncomplimentary comments about the College. The student said that he saw this essay as a 'a bit of a warm-up'. He saw interviewing 'as a bit of an art and a bit of a science' although he might not use that as a title. He thought he 'might use some quote' as a title. The supervisor muttered something which was difficult to catch, both for the student and on the tape, about 'what you bring and what you learn'. Despite the student trying to get in here she continued by reflecting on, and telling him about, the nature of 'practice teaching'.

In the next exchange the student said he thought 'knowledge was skills plus being'. The supervisor said that it was important to consider 'having, being and doing components of learning'. The student asked about 'being' and was told that it was 'about the use of self in your work'.

The student talked about what he had read in this field and it becomes clear that this material is not yet well-assimilated and not very connected with his practice. A great deal of anxious laughter punctuates the next few exchanges. The supervisor seems a bit lost, and finds it difficult to follow the student's arguments, but asks 'Do you mean being where the client is and giving space to them?' giving an illustration of this from her own work, which the student did not pick up on. He continues in the same way as before.

The supervisor says that 'The model is about discovering new bits of self' but when she gets no response quickly says 'I'm thinking out loud' . . . The student continues in the same rather lofty tones: 'When we are talking about self in modern psychology . . .' but this time the supervisor challenges whether the different points made were in fact not distinct, but were different levels of the same thing. The student continues, still in the same tone of voice, 'In philosophy, the self is ONE, in many of the ancient traditions . . .'

The supervisor tries another challenge: 'It sounds almost like a religion because you are so enthusiastic . . .' The supervisor is not sure of this ground at all and says rather defensively 'I've looked at things too, but not necessarily in such well worked-out ways' [sic]. She says 'Social work is about staying with people while they are going through bad things . . .'

The supervisor says 'I'd like to set the scene for the next session, and think about interviewing – how can we relate this to skills' [sic]. The student replies by linking back to the previous discussion, and says 'I actually believe there is *only one way* of interviewing, of being with someone . . . you are there and listening'. The supervisor picks up on 'only one way' by asking about 'the doing bit of being'. The student says 'knowledge arises from being'. The supervisor tentatively challenges . . .

After this, the student says 'They [clients] are different from other people . . . (and this legitimates) . . . a more directive response'. The supervisor challenges the student, and asks about integrating theory and practice. The student says that 'practice is the application of theory', but the supervisor says she thinks that 'theories are not just descriptions of practice . . . they are conceptualizations'.

The session finishes after an exchange in which the student says 'I don't quite understand what is bothering you' and the supervisor responds in terms of him being able to generalize so that he can use his experience.

This session contains within it material which is susceptible to many levels of description and analysis. Simply reviewing the content shows that it moves from initial scene-setting, and agenda-building exchanges, to discussion of what the student should do in one of the cases he is being asked to work with, and to the longer discussions about the team, and the student's essay topic.

This content-focused account is inadequate in understanding the subtleties of the interactions in the supervision session. The supervisor is concerned to appear as a good teacher, to be business-like, and to set the tone for the placement. The student is initially very passive, and does not respond very much, although after the discussion about how the team members get on he becomes more assertive. Subsequently, when he is given more opportunity to talk, he discusses his recent reading, which has clearly had an important influence on him.

But it is in the interaction between the two participants that some of the most revealing material emerges. At the beginning, the supervisor is clearly in control, and sets out the ground-rules, and her expectations. In doing so, she echoes the terms of the contract for the placement by emphasizing what she expects to happen. Although the student is invited to say whether he wants to bring anything to the session, he apparently does not understand this to be a coded way of valuing his contribution to his own learning.

The supervisor then tells the student what he should do in the case she has passed to him. There seems to be very much a pattern of *instruction*, in a *hierarchical relationship*, which does not seem to start by identifying the student's competence, and what needs to be learned in the placement.

The supervisor seems concerned to get her perceptions of the team meeting confirmed by the student, but despite considerable pressure, the student resists and eventually is explicit about his lack of interest in that discussion.

The opportunities afforded by the case discussion, and the talk about social work teams include the student directly referring to his previous experience, but on each occasion the supervisor does not use this as teaching material. The next part of the session, discussing the student's planned essay, includes the student trying to talk about his ideas and experience, but the supervisor tells him about the importance of valuing the student's previous experience, and what he can contribute to supervision sessions and to his own learning. The timing here suggests that she recognizes the importance of using the student's previous experience, but she does not actually do this.

It is possible to interpret some of the transactions as attempts to deal with the uncertainty which goes along with the establishing of a new supervisory relationship; but it is also possible to see the interactions as attempts by the supervisor to establish authority and power, in the supervisory relationship and in the area team as a whole. It is evident that the student does not go along with this entirely.

The purpose of their meeting is for the student to learn. The supervisor, though, seems concerned with her role as a supervisor, with an emphasis on her teaching rather than on the student's learning, and on her need to super-vise, i.e. to 'over-see' his work on behalf of the agency.

Later, after the student will not support her in the team politics, she swings towards greater passivity and uncertain challenges to the over-generalizations drawn from his reading. The student also appears to have a clear conception of teaching and learning, and of the relationship of theory to practice; this perhaps explains why he did not respond to the question about whether he had 'anything to bring to the session'. He did not seem to expect that this would be how the teaching and learning was going to be conducted.

Some other interesting findings emerge from this first session, about the notion of social work practice each has – the supervisor appears to think that there is a right way to approach the cases she has passed on to the student, and gives him a clear indication of what this will be by advising in some detail what she thinks he should do. Similarly, the student believes there is only one way to work with clients (by 'being' with them), although it is a different 'right way' from that of the supervisor.

The main themes and issues in this first session become recurrent elements for the entire placement, although they were not so obvious to the participants at the time. They are examined in the following sections, after which their contribution to defining the next stage of the study is described.

3.2.2   Single case study – sessions three to five

The following accounts are selected to illustrate and develop the issues raised in the first session, and some further issues, notably assessment.

In *Session Three*, the language used still seems to be rather formal and stilted. The supervisor continues, in this session, to offer direct advice on whom to contact and what to do about the cases. Because this does not seem to fit with what the student is expecting, she reiterates it, together with some generalizations to justify why she is doing so but the student does not respond. Eventually she asks 'What would have happened to this case in your old office?' and is told, after a long pause, that 'It would have been dealt with on a duty basis', and that 'It is unlikely that it would have been allocated' . . .

This exchange is followed by a long and detailed 'rehearsal' of the forthcoming interview. The supervisor asks very specific questions like 'Is there anything you'd like to say to her?' and 'Why is she unable to come in to the office . . . ?' It appears that the student eventually acquiesces, and joins in with the rehearsal, but he shows little enthusiasm for it.

The break caused by changing to the other side of the tape changes the tone of the discussion, which gives the chance to raise other issues and the supervisor asks what the student has done since leaving school. The student says he 'wanted to do something practical' and so dropped out of his degree course. He got a job, via an employment agency, to work with children in outer London; and then decided he 'wanted to live somewhere more rural' and moved to working in a large county authority. There he worked with handicapped children and later moved to a hospital which was 'more therapeutic'. He then went into teacher training because he wanted to do 'special teaching' in a residential school where his role would be 'not just educational but therapeutic'.

He was asked why he had dropped out of that and after a long silence he suggested that 'teaching was not enough'. He went on to say that he had fallen out with someone who was 'hot on the more formalized aspects'. The supervisor asked a lot of questions about the kind of educational model which they used although the student didn't seem clear what she was asking about.

It seems during this discussion that the supervisor is trying to find out more about the student, but the history of his life experiences is gathered by asking the kinds of questions social workers ask clients about their lives. This approach does not elicit very much about the student's expectations of learning in the placement. What is evident, however, is that he is not finding this supervisor very easy, and she acknowledged in a telephone conversation shortly afterwards that she was becoming 'increasingly bothered about him' and, because he didn't seem to respond to her teaching, that he 'might be a failing student'.

By *Session Five* these patterns seem to be well-established: the student at one point is talking about the cases he carried in his previous team and describes his work as 'picking up the pieces' and he apparently means that his work was fragmented, and episodic, and included few opportunities for sustained work in depth. The supervisor responded a little differently, by seeing the problem as 'coping with the bits and pieces left by others in the team'.

Her preoccupation with what is going on in her present team draws the supervisor away from the problem the student is describing, and she does not make use of the material he is providing. I began to wonder at this stage of the placement why an experienced and well-educated social worker, who was well-motivated and keen to improve her supervisory skills, was not managing to make effective contact with this student – and, conversely, why a student who was bright and experienced (in his pre-course social work) was not able to use what this supervisor was keen to offer. It seemed as though they were moving towards each other on parallel but separate lines, and missing each other.

One previous situation which the student described was a case where the mother 'had been diagnosed as a schizophrenic' which the student seemed ready to talk more about, describing a focus in supervision on 'practicalities . . . it didn't involve me making connections . . . there wasn't so much dialogue . . . as in this [placement] supervision . . .'

The supervisor was very concerned about how these cases were managed in his old team, rather than what the student did, or what he had learned from them.

The student says he is 'not used to clients valuing my existence as a worker', and that he feels his previous workload had been biased too heavily in that direction [i.e. working with reluctant clients]. The supervisor generalizes and talks about 'casework and change'. She is doing some direct teaching but the student does not seem very interested in this. He responds by saying that he is 'not sure how to measure being helpful'.

A discussion about how people change continues until the supervisor challenges the student that if the model is good enough for him, why is it not equally so for clients. The student flounders, and the supervisor jumps in to explain further what she means . . . then she challenges again, rescues, explains and challenges again, but in a different way. This time she says 'and . . .' after his comment and leaves a hanging silence which the student does not fill. The supervisor eventually comes in and asks directly 'When were you last conscious of having changed?' and follows this by 'Let's be specific'.

This is the first major challenge during the placement which the supervisor sustains, rather than allowing more general and abstract discussions to distract her.

She presses further: 'Have you changed in the weeks you have been here?' and the student at last talks in detail about changes – although they are changes in his clients and not changes for him. This eventually drifts off again into a discussion about self-awareness when the supervisor asks 'Why do you want to be good at it (i.e. self-awareness)?' and the student replies 'because it is about maturity'.

These sessions are characterized by a pattern of two well-meaning and well-intentioned individuals repeatedly failing to make effective contributions to supervision and having recurrent difficulties and misunderstandings. The supervisor is beginning to have doubts about whether the student will pass, and is further drawn into directive teaching. This view was apparently based as much on his performance in supervision as with his clients, since she had no direct evidence of the latter. This raises some interesting side issues about the need for direct evidence in evaluating the performance of social work students.

Some of this becomes more explicable when we consider the concerns the supervisor has which lead her to emphasize her teaching role. The case discussions exemplify this, because the student describes events and experiences which could be raw material for helping him to recognize patterns in his work and in his learning, but the supervisor becomes more and more caught up in managing the cases from an agency point of view.

She acknowledged later, in a taped interview, that she clearly wanted to 'teach', and to value his experience, but the response to her teaching made her concerned about his competence, and the cycle was repeated.

3.2.3 Single case study – session six onwards

In *Session Six*, there was a substantial discussion about a case the student was working with. The supervisor says that 'it is important to be clear what is going on in this family'. The supervisor asked what the student 'felt about what was going on in the family' but was misheard and had to say it again.

This happens several times in the course of the discussion – the student cannot 'hear' what is being asked about his involvement in the family situation, and what he feels about it. He does not quite understand, it seems, why the supervisor should be very interested in this.

There was another detailed rehearsal of what the student should do in a forthcoming interview. This seems largely about taking a social history from a client, and how to get other similar material . . . She goes on to make a link to the past experience of the student but then is a bit thrown by a very specific question from the student about 'whether you should take a family social history whilst the daughter is in the room?'

The supervisor begins to develop some connections between the student's current cases and his past experience. However, the student appears to want to find out right and wrong ways to do things like taking a family history. The student may be a cue-seeker, responding to how the supervisor has been teaching.

They turn to a discussion about a possible new case, and the student says he would like to do 'family work'. The supervisor says rather quickly and defensively that there is a lot going on in the families of his existing cases.

This reiterates the challenges and patterns from earlier in the placement, about what the student thinks of the cases he has been given (which would not have justified allocation at all in his last office).

The session turned to considering a study day for supervisors and students locally which was going to be held in the area office soon. The purpose of the day would be to allow discussion about interviewing skills and study skills. The supervisor talked about the teaching of social work at the college – which the student thought was superficial. He also said he could not see the relevance of the sociology teaching, but the discussion petered out because the supervisor seemed quiet and subdued during this. Her comments were closed and a little dogmatic. She seemed pre-occupied.

It is clear that the session is about to end when the supervisor asks for feedback on how the placement is going and on their supervisory relationship. The student is a bit perplexed and eventually says that he thinks the supervisor 'blows hot and cold'. It seems that the supervisor might have wanted to develop this discussion, about her view of his competence, but in the event does not do so.

The next two tapes focus on *Sessions Eight and Nine* which were primarily concerned with the interim assessment report which would be sent to the college. They cover much of the same ground and raise similar issues.

The student sounds noticeably more sure of himself in these tapes. There is still a considerable focus on a caseload-management type of supervision. By contrast the supervisor is more unsure of herself, is talking rather a lot, and intruding into what the student is saying, by cutting across him with pressure to emphasize her own viewpoint. Later, we see where some of this pressure is coming from, as the supervisor tries to set up a position where she can let him know her doubts in the interim assessment.

They begin to talk about assessment but it is not immediately clear that the student realizes that the supervisor is talking about assessing *him* rather than *his* assessment of the family in the case they are discussing. The supervisor does not let the student finish many of his sentences around this point, and often jumps into the pauses by finishing sentences for him.

The rest of the session is a discussion about the concept 'insight,' which both seem to think is equated with intellectual understanding. Neither suggests referring to the literature to support their view, and neither suggests that they could check this out for next time. It is perhaps typical of the insularity and introspection of supervision in this placement.

For the following session, also on assessment, the student has been asked to write something about his performance on the placement so far. He says 'It is difficult to write about yourself . . .' but is interrupted and the discussion turns to being a debate about the relative merits of 'being subjective versus being objective'.

The student talks much more about himself in describing his work in this session, which seems to have been prompted by writing the self-evaluative piece. He says that he is more relaxed than at the beginning of the placement. He linked this to his earlier rather unsatisfactory educational experiences. The supervisor turns this into a discussion about her authority and how adults learn, which deters the student from continuing.

Throughout this discussion, there is a pattern of interruptions by the supervisor and shifts by her towards making more general points about how adults learn. She describes the 'importance of helping them to value and use their own experience', but her interruptions and instruction (talking about learning) make it difficult to use what the student is offering.

Over the next month, only two supervision sessions occurred (because the supervisor took two weeks holiday as part of her annual leave) and only one of these was recorded. The patterns described above continued in this session, but without the pressure of the interim assessment the supervisor seemed less intrusive. Having not been explicit about her concerns, the gap caused by her holiday has given the student a little more space.

The *penultimate session* demonstrates this. This tape has a distinctly more relaxed tone for both supervisor and the student. The latter felt free enough to compare this supervisor with his previous one. The previous supervisor was 'more supportive' whilst this one was 'more challenging'.

The session indeed shows the supervisor as more relaxed and supportive, and she clearly continues to attach a great deal of significance to the nature and quality of their supervisory relationship as an indicator of progress for the student.

The student had produced another good piece of written work for the final evaluation, and he himself made a good link between 'use of self' with clients and in reflective writing. He began to talk about 'the value of being human in your work', but the supervisor struck a cautionary note about 'the importance of holding off your own needs with clients and not imposing', but the student pursued the point and 'admitted' that there were times when he used his own life experience with clients. He gave an example of the impending birth of his own child.

The student here indicated not only his increasing confidence and competence, but also gave evidence that some of his earlier responses in supervision indicated his cue-consciousness in responding to his supervisor's lead. Now, nearly at the end of the placement, he is able to 'own up' to what he has actually been doing with his clients, which includes some (appropriate) personal involvement in his work.

> The student had also taped an interview with a family and brought it to supervision, even though he felt it had not been a very good interview, and had offered it to the supervisor for comment. The supervisor is supportive to these moves which certainly seem to be associated with the lifting of the pressure of assessment, because she has decided he should pass. The entire tone of the final sessions is in marked contrast to the early tapes reflecting a different balance between student and supervisor. Some of this seems to have been prompted by the student fending for himself whilst the supervisor was on leave.

The selection of material from these sessions has been increasingly narrowed. In this way, it is possible to discern those areas where there has been movement on the part of the supervisor and student.

Some of this selection has been informed by the initial sessions of the placement itself, but material has also been selected to give descriptive evidence of the problems identified in the supervision literature. Included in that is the supervisor's concern that the student might not pass because of the difficulties in the supervisory relationship.

In looking at the performance of the supervisor, it is evident that she was at a critical stage not only in the development of her supervisory skills, but more importantly, in her conception of the teaching and learning processes in professional education. As a result of being encapsulated at this point of transition by the study, some of the limitations of her approach are more starkly represented than if we had studied the previous or next placement in which she was involved.

It is relatively easy, by observation of the sessions, and in interpretations with the benefit of hindsight, to point to the limitations of the approach she was employing. Had she been less explicitly concerned with improving her *teaching* skills, and demonstrating these to the student and the researcher, she may have been able to relax and give the student the space he used profitably towards the end of the placement. After reading this account, she confirmed that view.

3.3   An overview of the initial data collection

This chapter began with the intention of gathering data on the teaching and learning processes involved in social work supervision. The questionnaire showed that supervisors construe supervision in different ways and, related to these conceptions of the teaching and learning processes, they had difficulties when working with students who did not learn in the expected ways. These findings suggest that the matching of the styles, or approaches, of teachers and learners would be an important way to make supervision sessions more effective.

The single case-study also showed that different conceptions of the teaching and learning processes underlay at least some of the interactive patterns described. In addition to the issues of learning styles and teaching styles, there were some indications of a close connection between how the supervisor approaches teaching and her expectation of whether the student was likely to pass the placement. Assessment seemed to constrain, and then free, the participants in this placement to the extent that the supervisor became much more directive when she found the student not behaving in expected ways in supervision. Subsequently, when things were going better in supervision, she felt he should pass, and the student responded by involving himself more in his work and in his learning. This seems to have been a mutually reinforcing cycle of events.

This placement emphasises the importance of the teacher, and what is to be taught, so that when the student does not respond in the expected way, it is assumed that he is somehow failing, and the task of the teacher is to help him with these presumed learning difficulties.

The limitation of the classical model of supervision is that it focuses attention on the individual, not on the nature of the interactions between individuals. It is important not to make the same mistake when looking at the reports of this case study. It is not helpful to blame the supervisor for failing to do things differently, especially when she herself was changing and developing as a teacher. To account for these experiences adequately, we need to look at the interactions between the supervisor and the student, at the patterns in these transactions, and then try to explain them in terms which illumine rather than obscure the interaction. There is a need, therefore, to formulate concepts which describe these events as interactions, and which can account for patterns which may be sustained over a considerable period of time, and which may change or develop.

In summary, the data reported so far have emphasized the importance of the key issues identified: the use of language; the need to look at learning styles and stages; the impact of the conceptions those involved have of teaching and learning; the importance of assessment; and the significance of the duration of the supervisory experience which allows development and change in the patterns of interaction in supervision. These issues are also dealt with in other research into student learning in higher education, so before gathering further data, an exploration of that literature was made.

4

Adult Learning Research

4.1 Adults as learners

Two areas of relevant work were found in the literature: one with its roots in a broader tradition of adult education, and literacy, seeing the importance of education as a political tool; the other is derived from research into adult learning in higher education.

It should be emphasized that the literature reviewed here has been carefully selected for its contribution to a study of professional education. It does not purport to be a comprehensive review of research in cognitive psychology – although much of that literature was searched and evaluated for its relevance to the study.

Earlier the social work literature review, and the accounts of supervision, have shown the essential paradox between hierarchical supervisory models (based on notions of expertise to be imparted), and those which might encourage adult learners to make meanings from their own experiences.

Carl Rogers (1961) describes the importance of learner-centred education:

> It seems to me that anything that can be taught to another is relatively inconsequential, and has little or no significant influence on behaviour . . . the only learning which significantly influences behaviour is self-discovered, self-appropriated learning . . . [and] such self-discovery learning, truth that has been personally appropriated and assimilated in experience, can not be directly communicated to another . . .

Eight years later, Rogers (1969) draws some conclusions from these speculations, which he reports as dating originally from his writings in 1952:

> Learning is facilitated when the student participates responsibly in the learning process. When he chooses his own direction, helps to discover his own learning resources, formulates his own problems, decides his own course of action, lives with the consequences of these choices, then significant learning is maximised.

If learner-centred models contradict the traditional approaches to supervision, then the predominance and persistence of the latter must be explained. In particular, one must try to understand why social caseworkers and some in other professions see in the social casework supervision process a model which represents a level of refinement others should follow. In the same year that Rogers was setting out the characteristics of student-centred learning, Austin (1952) began the first paper in a collection on supervision with the following:

> Supervision, as it has been developed in social work, is commanding respect in other professions as well as in social work education and training. Because in supervision the basic laws of learning have been applied in new and meaningful combinations, it is making a distinctive contribution to education methods. It has synthesised knowledge about intellectual processes from the educational field with knowledge about the emotional and social components in learning, derived from both psycho-analytic psychology and social work practice.

Here we see Austin describing 'basic laws of learning' as though they are immutable, and apply to *all* students and *all* teachers, at *all* times. Their value, and this is part of their persistence in social work education, is that they address the affective and behavioural components of learning-for-action, as well as the cognitive components of learning. The social casework model of supervision is attempting to contribute to the same processes (students' learning) as the models of student-centred learning espoused by Rogers but from a very different perspective – that of the teacher, and of the discipline.

There are other factors which contribute to the persistence of this model beyond its time and place of origin – and these include the political and power dimensions of the model. It persists because it is a politically powerful tool – it values the experience and knowledge of the teacher above that of the learner. Such teacher-centred models can be attractive and seductive to those who are relatively inexperienced as teachers, those who teach part-time, and infrequently (i.e. most social work supervisors) because they appear to bring certainty, order and control to what might otherwise be an unknown activity.

Smith (1977) discusses these kinds of political issues in a review of 'alternative' challenges to educational theory in unpublished or 'grey' literature. He describes Patton's challenge to Peters' view of education as initiation into worthwhile activities. These counter-culture perspectives of the 1960s provide a radical challenge to the essentially controlling and conservative functions of education in society. This is re-interpreted in the third world recognitions of the importance of literacy and the education of adults if oppression is to be resisted. Thus, Illich's notions of deschooling (1970) and Freire's radical prescription of liberation theology (1972) can be seen as general statements of the kinds of issues we can see reflected in a professional education which devalues the role that learners have to play in their own significant learning. Freire says (1972):

> Liberating education consists in acts of cognition, not transferrals of information.

> A careful analysis of the teacher-student relationship at any level . . . reveals its fundamentally narrative character. This relationship involves a narrating subject [the teacher] and patient, listening objects [the students] . . . Narration . . . turns them into 'containers', into 'receptacles' to be 'filled' by the teacher.

This view is echoed in the literature on professionalization which challenges the power relationships between professionals and their clients – not only in their direct service relationship, but also in the ways that professionals control the definition of problems, and access to the professional classes to deal with problems they have defined (Illich 1977):

> Educators, for instance, now tell society what must be learned, and are in a position to write off as valueless what has been learned outside of school . . . Today, doctors and social workers – as formerly only priests and jurists – gain legal power to create the need that, by law, they alone will be allowed to satisfy . . .
> Professionals assert secret knowledge about human nature, knowledge which only they have the right to dispense. They claim a monopoly over the definition and the remedies needed.

It is in the light of such an analysis of professional power that we can view the moves over the last forty or fifty years to professionalize social work. In parallel, the resistance of supervisors and tutors to challenges to their power and authority over the learning process of intending social workers is made more explicable. As Humpty Dumpty says: 'The question is, which is to be master, that's all' (Carroll 1877).

The autobiographical account of supervision, whilst the author was a student, showed how conflicts about control of student learning was an important source of the continuing problems, and that this finding was replicated in the single case study.

What Knowles (1978) says about adult learning is largely congruent with Illich and Freire in emphasizing the importance of andragogical models, which give responsibility to students for their own learning. Knowles (1972) addressed these issues more specifically in relation to social work education when he spoke at the Annual Conference of the Council on Social Work Education (broadly the American equivalent of CCETSW) in New York:

> We have finally really begun to absorb into our culture the ancient insight that the heart of education is learning, not teaching, and so our focus has started to shift from what the teacher does to what happens to the learners.

The questionnaire exercise in this study showed that those who were more experienced (student unit supervisors) sometimes had conceptions of the adult learning process which aspired (implicitly and explicitly), to be andragogical models; but some had difficulty coping with students who were unwilling or unable to learn in the ways expected of them. Those supervisors seemed to assume that 'starting from the experience of the learner' would inevitably allow students to make such a contribution. The questionnaire findings and the single case study show that this is an untenable assumption, since some students either did not expect learning to take place in that way, or were not yet ready for it to do so.

Attempts to build conceptual frameworks which arise from the synthesis of educational theory and current social work practice, as well as the political and institutional contexts of the 1980s rather than the 1940s and 1950s, need to consider recent insights drawn from research into adult learning; then the data gathered can be carefully examined to see whether such concepts illumine or give meaning to those interactions.

It is therefore helpful to see the discussion in this section as being primarily concerned with presage factors, including setting up a climate or culture to promote student-centred learning (Biggs 1978 and 1985), and as pre-cursors of the teaching-learning interaction. In placements this means creating a learning milieu for the placement, negotiating a contract, and so on. As part of the context of learning they can pre-dispose the possibility of active learning by the student, but they do not necessarily bring it about. Six of the seven principles which Knowles espouses are not directly related to teaching and learning processes themselves.

To understand the relationship between teaching and learning, and the influence of the context, it is necessary to look closely at learners' perceptions of the learning task in a particular context, and their conceptions of the learning required to accomplish it. To do this, a different tradition must be explored, that of research into student learning in higher education.

4.2   Adult learning research

The literature reported in this section is work which had been completed and published at this point in the study. More recent research, undertaken and published during the period of this study, is included in Chapter 7, in the light of the findings of this research. This allows the developing conceptions of the teaching and learning processes to be reported as they occurred, without reinterpretation in the light of subsequently-generated insights from other research.

The focus of research into adult learning has changed substantially over the past ten years. In social work education we are used to thinking about the need to individualize learning, and to look at the individual student's learning – even if, as we have seen, that focus is often expressed in terms derived from psycho-social casework.

However, research into learning in higher education has only recently given attention to the learner's own experience of learning, and to learning in natural settings. This has allowed more attention to be given to the impact of the context (including teaching and assessment as well as location) on the nature and quality of student learning.

Much of the early learning research concentrated on reproductive, memory-based learning, like memorising nonsense symbols (Ebbinghaus 1885), rather than on significant, meaningful learning (Rogers 1969) or learning as a matter of constructing meaning (Ausubel 1968). To focus on meaningful, constructive learning, more recent work has used different methods, but they represent not only a shift of paradigm of methodology, but of perspective (Entwistle 1984):

> The new research paradigm switches perspective and so provides insights for the teacher which are not only firmly rooted in real-life situations in higher education, but are also more illuminating. They present a description of student learning from an unusual perspective – that of the student.

The first stage of the present study duplicated this shift by beginning with a focus on supervisors (in the questionnaire and the single case study) and moving towards increasing concern with the students' learning, and its relation to supervisors' teaching. Such a shift allows the interpretation and presentation of data as recognizable realities – which can have meaning to the students themselves, their teachers, and others in social work education.

This literature review is very selective, giving primary attention to the content of learning, the process of learning, the outcome of learning, the context in which the learning takes place, and the relationship between each of these aspects of learning. At the heart of much recent thinking are a series of studies undertaken at Göteborg (Gothenburg) Sweden, by Marton and his colleagues.

4.2.1   The seminal Göteborg studies

For more than ten years, the researchers at the University of Göteborg have been reporting their studies of approaches to, and outcomes of, learning for adult students. In the experimental studies (e.g. Marton and Saljo 1976a and 1976b; Saljo 1975) attention was given to how students had approached reading and answering questions on a set text. Marton and Saljo stress that they are interested in 'differences in what is learned rather than differences in how much is learned'. Wilson (1981) summarizes their method succinctly:

> The materials used have included edited chapters of books, newspaper articles and home produced papers of similar complexity. Average length is 3000 words. Samples are small, consisting of around 30 first year students, mostly girls, who are paid volunteers. No background information, personality or intellectual correlates are reported. The procedure adopted is for the student to study the set text, without time limit, in a one-to-one tape-recorded situation with the experimenter. She then answers oral and/or written questions about her understanding of the text, and gives an introspective account of how she read it . . . Long term recall is tested between five and seven weeks later.

The students' answers were assigned to categories by the experimenter and a colleague independently. Two main groups of responses, which seemed to be qualitatively different, were identified. In one group, there was concern to *remember the content* of the text. In the other, there was more concern with *principles and meaning*. These two levels of approach are qualitatively different – they are not simply ends of a continuum.

These two levels of approach are described by Marton *et al.* as the *surface* approach, and the *deep* approach, respectively. In the former, there is what they describe as a focus on the *sign*, and the latter on *what is signified* (or meant by the text).

It is interesting that in an early paper (Marton 1975) a distinction is made between those who are active in their learning, and those who passively experience learning as something that happens to them:

> For some, learning is the grasping of what the discourse is about, i.e. learning is learning *through* the discourse, and for others, learning is learning the discourse (i.e. memorising it). The former appear to experience an active role (i.e. learning is something they do); the latter appear not to do this (i.e. learning is something that happens to them).

This difference is another way of interpreting findings from the questionnaire exercise where some supervisors described important learning experiences requiring the involvement of a significant other person to help make sense of the experience. It may be that this group are those who expect to learn passively. Equally, the group who learnt through reflection on their own may well have expectations that they should be active in their learning. This distinction is explored in the next stage of data collection because the two approaches described may not be simply differences of *type*, but may represent different *stages of development* for individual learners as they take increasing responsibility for their own learning.

The Göteborg work offers much more than the simple distinction between 'deep' and 'surface' approaches to learning (and their relationship with active and passive learning). It also demonstrates that students' approaches to learning are closely related to the outcomes of that learning. Thus a *decision to adopt a surface approach rules out the possibility of a deep outcome* (i.e. understanding meaning) simply *because it was not being looked for, and was not seen as the purpose of the learning*. Students may change their approach in different circumstances, depending on their perceptions of the task. Marton and Saljo (1976a) make this clear:

> . . . the between group differences point out the clear modifiability and context-dependence of a person's conception of learning. In other words, learning seems to be defined differently depending on, for instance, anticipated task demands.
>
>   Students adopt an approach determined by their expectations of what is required of them.

Marton and Saljo also demonstrated that whilst none of those who had adopted a surface approach understood the author's argument, none of those who used a deep approach failed to achieve a good understanding of the argument. This is a very significant finding for all learning in higher education, especially in professional and vocational training, where students are expected not simply to reproduce ideas, but to be able to reflect on their usefulness, and make use of them in diverse practice situations.

If, however, deep outcomes are not intended (or more importantly, students perceive them not to be so) then it is unlikely that deep approaches will be used. In the single case study, the supervisor was concerned about the student's performance, and was drawn into a good deal of directive teaching. The student, who perhaps responded to his teacher's cues, was induced to use passive approaches to learning – i.e. learning which is derived from the knowledge and expertise of the teacher. The vital point which Marton makes, about the student not looking for 'deep' outcomes in his learning, because they were not asked for, can also be induced by teacher-centred, and directive kinds of teaching.

The findings from the Göteborg work are made more explicable by a study which looked at the importance of the learner's conception of the task in determining both the approach to learning and the outcome of that learning (Saljo 1975). Two questions which are of considerable relevance to this study are addressed: first, how to go about identifying and describing qualitative differences in learning (i.e. what is actually learned), rather than a quantifiable measure of learning, like examination results. The second is how these qualitative aspects of the learning process, and outcomes of learning, are affected by the nature of the assessment of that learning.

Saljo asked forty first year female students at University to read chapters from a textbook on education, and to prepare themselves to answer some questions afterwards. After each of the first two chapters, half of the students were asked one kind of question (the SL group), and half (the DL group) another kind. The first kind required close attention to the detail of the text, and were intended to induce reproductive, surface-level (SL) processing. The second kind of question was intended to induce deep-level (DL) processing by focusing upon the understanding of assumptions and ideas in the text which were the basis of the strengths and limitations of the author's arguments.

After reading a third chapter, both groups were tested with questions of both kinds, and they were required to recall the text and to summarize it in a few sentences. Saljo grouped the answers and the recall into categories which reflected different kinds of comprehension. The most superficial level involved simply *mentioning* a fact discussed by the author. At the next level were *descriptions of what was said* in the text. The third level was *relating the content of the text to its conclusions*.

Saljo reports that his subjects tried to adapt their learning towards the requirements of the questions – the SL group were all induced to look closely at the text itself in the following chapter. The DL group used two main strategies: one sub-group adopted the intended deep level strategy; the other sub-group 'technified' the task into simply producing the required skeleton summary without attempting any further analysis. Thus Saljo demonstrated a close connection between the approach to learning and the outcome of that learning, and he showed the direct influence of the form of assessment on the approaches students used.

Clearly, the implication of this work for looking at teaching and learning in supervision (and the impact of how learning is assessed), is that considerable attention should be given to these factors when looking at the contextual influences on teaching and learning interactions. Entwistle's (1977) comment should be noted:

> . . . over half the Swedish first-year students were classified as surface-processors, and a similar proportion has been reported in England.

Other work in Göteborg (Svensson 1976) has demonstrated essentially similar results from looking at everyday studying in normal coursework. An interesting finding from Svensson's work was the extent to which particular strategies were related to academic success. One would expect his finding that those who choose strategies which closely matched the examination requirements generally do better than where there is a mis-match. Svensson also showed that the amount of work undertaken by students was related to their learning approach – deep-level processors are better able to sustain high levels of study time throughout the term, whereas surface-level processing students showed a fall-off in the amount they worked as the term wore on.

The Göteborg work relates to other work in the field. Those students who are able to accurately identify the nature of the assessment task (e.g. cue-seekers – Miller and Parlett 1973) may be better able than other students to adjust their learning strategies to fit course assessment requirements.

The possibility of making such changes in approach assumes that learners have a choice of learning strategies available to them. A pre-condition of such choice is to recognize that there are diverse ways of approaching learning tasks in the first place. Such recognition also relies on the ability of the learner to discriminate accurately different kinds of learning requirements, which in turn is dependent upon the ability to conceive of 'learning' as including very different kinds of activity.

In the questionnaire exercise, supervisors were asked to describe what for them were significant learning experiences, and variations in those experiences were reported. However, it is possible to classify them on a rather different basis – one which relates to the learner's conceptions of learning itself. Those who have very narrow conceptions of what is involved in 'learning', are likely to see quite diverse learning tasks as requiring the same kind of approach; others who have broad conceptions of learning are more likely to be able to discriminate the requirements of a particular task accurately, and to respond with an appropriate learning approach.

Marton reports that it is easier to induce surface learning amongst those students who can employ deep strategies than vice versa. This finding can be accounted for by recognizing some students are versatile in having a repertoire of learning approaches; and that there are stages of development, of increasing versatility, through which adult learners pass.

Saljo has something further to offer in this connection, since he has reported work on levels of the learner's conception of learning (Saljo 1979). By describing and categorizing the replies he received to the question 'What do you mean by learning?', he identified five different conceptions:

Conception 1: Learning as the increase in knowledge . . . The main feature of this first category is its vagueness in the sense that what is given in the answers is merely a set of synonyms for the word learning . . .

Conception 2: Learning as memorising . . . the meaning of learning is to transfer units of information or pieces of knowledge, or what is commonly called facts, from an external source, such as a teacher or book, into the head . . .

Conception 3: Learning as the acquisition of facts, procedures etc which can be retained and/or used in practice . . .

Conception 4: Learning as the abstraction of meaning . . . compared to the two previous categories . . . the nature of what is learned is changed . . . learning is no longer conceived of as an activity of reproduction, but instead as a process of abstracting meaning from what you read and hear . . . The learning material is not seen as containing ready made knowledge to be memorised, but rather it provides the raw material or starting point for learning . . .

Conception 5: Learning as an interpretive process aimed at the understanding of reality . . . very similar to the previous one . . . (but) a further distinction is that some subjects emphasise that an essential element of learning is that what you learn should help you interpret the reality in which you live . . .

Conceptions Two and Three are reproductive conceptions, which constrain students to using surface approaches, comprise seeing learning as external, and something which happens to the student. The later conceptions (4 and 5) are constructive conceptions, allowing deep approaches which involve the learner actively in the process of learning – which is seen as construing meaning. Later, a further developmental model of how students experience their world, and their conceptions of learning, is described (Perry 1970).

The Göteborg studies help to identify a number of key elements of an exploration of teaching and learning in supervision, including:

differences in approaches to learning (surface and deep processing)

the relationship between approaches to learning and outcomes of learning

the impact of assessment on the approaches to, and outcomes of, learning

the importance of the learner's conceptions of learning in determining his ability to discriminate between various kinds of learning task, and his ability to use different approaches appropriate to the kinds of learning outcome required.

The Göteborg work clearly has much that is of value in looking at learning that demonstrably occurs, and the inter-play between the learning processes and the context of learning (which includes teaching and assessment, as well as the institutional contexts within which the learning takes place). It should be noted that none of it is drawn from professional or vocational training programmes.

The different levels of students' conceptions of learning identified by Saljo certainly help to identify the range of learning requirements imposed on students during social work training. Indeed, in most courses, there is ample evidence of all of these kinds of learning being implicitly or explicitly required during the course. Students who are versatile in their approaches to learning are likely to make the best use of the time available on social work (and other professional or vocational) courses by utilizing approaches which best suit a particular task, in a particular context.

The Göteborg work looks at learning from the learner's perspective. Part of that perspective will include students' perceptions of the teaching and assessment processes to which they are subjected. Particular attention will be paid in the next stage of data collection to the *impact on teaching and learning interactions of different levels of conception of learning held by students* and *those held by supervisors*.

Before leaving this section on the seminal Göteborg studies, it is useful to reflect on the use of language that work employs, and the language to be used in the rest of this book. I normally use the term 'style' to mean a general cognitive approach, and the term 'strategy' or 'approach' to describe how a student tries to learn a specific task. Because these Göteborg studies have profoundly altered how researchers look at student learning within higher education, the studies of others on more general differences in cognitive style are not detailed here. Bruner on focusing or scanning strategies of concept acquisition (1960); Witkin *et al.* (1977) on field-dependence and independence; Parlett (1970) on syllabus-bound and syllabus-free students; and Hudson (1966) on convergers and divergers have all contributed to this field. Dahlgren and Marton's (1978) reflection on this body of work is instructive:

> Whether these various dichotomies refer to different phenomena or to different aspects of the same phenomenon is an open question. We favour the second alternative. All the dichotomies seem to relate more or less directly to two different conceptions of learning, namely learning as a transmission of unrelated 'bits of knowledge' on the one hand, and learning as a change in one's conception of some aspect of reality on the other.

Equally, Saljo's more recent (1987) caution about adult learning research is apposite:

> Looking today across the various branches of research that deal with such essential human phenomena as thinking and learning, the uninitiated but inquisitive novice is bound to experience considerable confusion. A process of continuous proliferation of subcommunities of researchers with their own paradigms of thought and accompanying vocabularies characterises

the development over past decades . . . [and we] can find that their glitter is fading when tested against the multi-faceted and complex reality of real-life cognitive activity.

4.2.2   Some research in Britain

The Göteborg studies look at natural or naturalistic learning, based on the ways in which students approach complex reading tasks. Over the same period, work was going on in Britain which had a rather different base, with roots in a different tradition. Pask and his associates have looked at ways of externalizing the internal processes (or learning strategies) students use in complex learning tasks. Some of Pask's early work was in the area of man-machine interaction, and some of the work is reported in journals in that field. In the educational literature there are references to the difficulty of understanding Pask's work, and papers by others to describe and explain it (e.g. Entwistle 1977 and 1978).

The difficulty seems to come about for two main reasons. One is that Pask uses language which has everyday usage and meaning (e.g. 'conversation') in quite special, and rather unusual, ways. The other reason is the artificiality of the complex tasks he devised. Whilst these exercises are free from contamination by previous knowledge, they fit uneasily into a growing tradition of research into learning in its natural environment. Pask's exercises are much less accessible than experimental presentations of everyday tasks like reading a set text. His exercises are also difficult to score, and therefore difficult to replicate (Laurillard 1978).

Pask and Scott (1972 and 1973) sought to find ways of 'mapping' students' learning strategies as they approached a learning task. They devised a computer program which could record the patterns by which the student 'interrogated a knowledge structure' (i.e. tried to learn about it, in a set task). Further work involving the learning of fictitious taxonomies reinforced their findings of two types of learning strategy, which Pask calls *holist* and *serialist*.

In these latter exercises some students seemed to focus on a small section of the overall taxonomy, and learn (i.e. memorize) the information they discovered in that area. They seemed relatively uninterested in the relationships of one sub-species to other sub-species. They were more concerned with 'local' learning. These subjects are exhibiting a *serialist* strategy.

Another group of the students seemed more interested in an overall understanding of the structure of the taxonomy, and of the hierarchical relationships between sub-species, combined usually with rather less detailed knowledge of individual sub-species. This 'global' approach to learning is described by Pask as a *holist* strategy. This task was used with all subjects in the next stage of the present study.

Pask and Scott have demonstrated these strategies through a range of complex learning tasks, and have claimed that the approaches are consistent for individual subjects across a number of tasks. This stability of approach is the subject of some discussion in the literature, but there is general acceptance of their findings that *when teaching is offered in ways which matched a preferred learning strategy, performance is much enhanced*; and *when teaching and learning approaches are mis-matched, there are significantly less good results* (Pask and Scott 1972).

Pask made use of a 'teachback' technique, where students are asked to teach the topic back to the instructor; he says that when complete mastery of the subject is achieved, then the student can be considered versatile in his learning. There are aspects of versatility unanswered in Pask's work which are of interest in social work education. In particular, at any one point in a social work course, or over the course as a whole, students may be expected to be able to demonstrate serialist strategies in relation to some parts of the curriculum (e.g. legislative provision) whilst at the same time demonstrating holist strategies (e.g. to integrate a complex set of inter-disciplinary materials with their practice experience in a single large case-study).

Attention could usefully be given in selection, in curriculum design, in teaching and assessment, to the kinds of learning strategies students need to use in order that they might accomplish the required learning tasks. As in the Göteborg work, Pask distinguishes levels of complexity in learners' conceptions of the learning task. Pask's categories, *comprehension learning* and *operation learning* reflect these differences, and their relation to holist and serialist strategies:

> . . . holist or serialist strategies . . . are thus insufficiently refined to account for learning in general. Holism and serialism appear to be extreme manifestations of more fundamental processes . . . (of comprehension learning and operation learning, respectively).

The extent to which students can be taught (or induced) to change their approach to learning was considered by Pask (1976a and 1976b) when he showed that learners can be taught to use particular strategies over short periods, but as Wilson (1981) reports, it seems easier to induce serialist strategies for those who have previously demonstrated holist approaches than vice-versa. These findings point towards the notion that operation and comprehension learning might be stage-related, rather than simply different types of approach, because it may be easier to return, or revert, to an earlier (serialist) strategy than to induce the growth necessary to demonstrate a later (holist) one. These findings are similar to the Göteborg findings that it is easier to induce surface learning in those who have demonstrated deep approaches than vice versa. This issue is considered in more detail in the next section.

Holist and serialist strategies are seen by Pask to be associated with levels of uncertainty and ambiguity which a learner can tolerate whilst undertaking the learning task. Holist strategies are associated with being able to take risks and tolerate uncertainty, and to maintain a number of possible hypotheses during the interrogation of the materials. For those adopting serialist strategies, a narrower focus and single hypothesis is chosen. Certainty and security for the learner, without fear of failure, are more likely to be conducive to the development of holist strategies. Supervisors who wish to encourage holist approaches will need to create a climate which is perceived as supportive to risk-taking by students. A number of instances demonstrating this were found in the case examples reported later in Chapters 5 and 6.

Equally, the context of learning, or at least the learner's perception of it, can constrain his approaches to learning. Laurillard (1978) reports a study of the relationship between some of the cognitive and contextual factors in student learning. She replicates some earlier research, including that of Pask, and of Marton, and tries to relate those methods to 'real learning situations i.e. learning tasks that students engage in as part of their academic coursework.' She considers case-examples of individual students and demonstrates:

> . . . that a student's approach to a task is partly dependent on his perception of that task, and on his perceptions of the circumstances in which he is doing it.

Her work demonstrates that deep and surface processing, and operation and comprehension learning, also describe characteristics of students' learning in their normal coursework, but they do not discriminate consistently between students. Instead, students are seen to use different approaches in different contexts. She offers a model which summarizes and accounts for her findings, and points to the importance of the learners' perceptions of the task as factors determining their approaches to learning, i.e. that learning styles are both content- and context-dependent:

> . . . Pask has identified two different styles of learning, comprehension and operation, but in order to make use of this, it is important to establish the conditions under which they occur, and the major factors that affect them. It is not sufficient to know that they exist – we must also discover under what circumstances they exist.

The value of her model is in suggesting a way of integrating the work of Marton with that of Pask. Whilst some have assumed that they may be describing much the same phenomena in student approaches to learning, Laurillard helpfully distinguishes them:

> . . . as describing different levels of the process of learning . . . A simple measure of the amount of operation or comprehension learning a student uses is not a measure of his level of understanding. The two together are a necessary but not sufficient condition for understanding. Thus deep level processing is characterised by some form of productive thinking and probably relates to what Pask defines as 'versatility' . . . (i.e. both operation and comprehension learning).

Throughout the discussions of this research in Britain and in Sweden, questions have been raised about whether the differences described are essentially differences of *type* or of *stage*, or both. Some American work illumines questions about developmental stages for adult learners.

4.2.3   Some American research

Perry's work (1970) is derived from interviews carried out at Harvard and Radcliffe, over three periods from 1954 onwards. It is based on unstructured interviews of about an hour in length, in each of students' four years at college. Perry's methodology involves the reading of transcripts of interviews, and looking for patterns and themes to emerge from them. His work is composed of substantial amounts of these qualitative data, together with a developmental scheme of the moral and intellectual development of students. It is reassuring, to those who carry out such qualitative studies, that the initial research related only to seventeen students, and that validation of the findings is based on a follow-up in 1962 and 1973 of a total of seventy students. Therefore in the next stage of collecting data it was important to ensure the quality and depth of the material (and its validity, derived from the methods used to interpret the findings), rather than simply dealing with larger samples.

Perry provides a detailed account of nine stages through which students pass, and provides examples which show the ebb and flow of movement which allows regression to earlier stages, and for some, sidings from the main route. There has been debate about whether the nine stages are normal development for all students. In describing the scheme here, attention will be concentrated upon some particularly relevant dimensions: students' conceptions of knowledge; their attitudes to authority; and their ideas about their own role in learning. These link closely, of course, to the work reported above.

Perry's scheme begins with students holding a polarized view of Right and Wrong, at Position One, where it is believed that Right Answers exist, and that they are known to Experts who are in Authority. In Position Two, students begin to recognize diversity of views, which they account for by believing that poorly-qualified authorities do not know the Answers, or they see expressions of diversity as exercises 'so that we can learn to find The Answer for ourselves'. Position Three is where the students accept that diversity exists, and see uncertainty as legitimate, but only because Authorities have not found the Answer yet. These first three positions are connected by a continuing belief in Right Answers, known to Authority, even in the face of increasing evidence of diversity.

The next three stages are about students recognizing that all knowledge and values are relativistic, and context-dependent. Position Four sees the student either perceiving legitimate uncertainty as widespread – 'everyone has their own opinion' – or he discovers qualitative, contextual reasoning (but only as a special case of 'what They want'). Thus whilst doubts about whether Right Answers exist have begun to creep in, it is still assumed that teachers are in Authority positions in relation to students' learning. Perry calls Position Five a stage of revolution, where all knowledge is recognized as relativistic, and the interpretation of what is 'known' is dependent upon context, and the frameworks used. Position Six is where the student realizes that he needs to make some form of personal, individual commitment (as distinct from an unquestioning belief in external Certainty).

The final three stages (Positions Seven, Eight and Nine) reflect students seeing a need to make personal commitments to particular value-positions, to begin to make them, and to take responsibility for them, consequently seeing a mature identity reflected in the positions adopted.

Perry reported in 1977 that he could find fewer instances of students entering college below Position Five than in 1954. Laurillard (1978) equally found that students in her sample 'expressed implicit theories of knowledge which were relativistic', but she did find evidence of changes, during the course, of the way students related to their teachers (by taking increasing responsibility for their own learning). She showed that although they might be at Five, or beyond, in some aspects of their development, beginning students in higher education had not always reached that stage.

It is clear from Perry's scheme that students' conceptions of learning tasks will be influenced by their position on the scale. Those with conceptions of single, right answers known to an authority-teacher are more likely to use surface-reproductive strategies, and to be relatively passive in their approaches to learning. Those who see knowledge as contextual and relativistic have abandoned the position of teachers as experts, and they can take increasingly active responsibility for their own learning, using deep-constructive approaches.

The work of Pask and the Göteborg group strongly associates approaches to learning with developing conceptions of the learning process. The implications of these three strands of work (Swedish, British, and American) for the focus and design of the rest of this study are considered in the next section.

4.3   Some implications of the adult learning research

Much of the work reported in this chapter has approached the problem of externalizing and making sense of adults' learning by identifying specific tasks in which some students demonstrate differences of approach and outcome. These differences are seen to be related to differences in conceptions of learning itself, which may reflect not only differences in type of approach to learning, but also differences in stage of development *as a learner*.

What began as a study of the literature to explore the impact of matching and mis-matching of teaching and learning styles has shown that such questions can only be considered alongside the conceptions teachers and learners have of the learning process. Thus, in trying to interpret data in the following sections, the *inter-relationships of style and stage* must be carefully considered in explaining patterns of interaction in supervision.

The data reported so far have demonstrated the need for interactive interpretations of the experiences. In collecting further data about teaching and learning in supervision, there is a need to gather descriptive data of events in supervision, and the meanings the participants attach to those events, so reflecting the conceptions they have of the learning process. This points to the use of interviews, to discuss these issues, and to follow up issues raised in the single case study and the questionnaire. The possibility of gathering related data about each placement to confirm or develop the interview material would not be ruled out.

It was also decided to use an external measure of learning style, based on established exercises or techniques, to use alongside the qualitative data. The Clobbits exercise developed by Pask had the advantage of being virtually unknown in the social work field, so there would be little effect on the results derived from previous knowledge. It was administered concurrently with interviews in the next stage. The version used was part of an Open University module designed to allow self-administration (Holloway 1977).

The exercise attempts to externalize learning processes by mapping routes used by students to learn a fictitious taxonomy as they gathered information presented on separate cards. The cards are grouped into various kinds of information. The steps taken are seen as indicative of strategies of learning. The results from this exercise have been detailed elsewhere (Gardiner 1987c) so here their contribution to the study is summarized.

The value of using the Clobbits exercise lies as much in its contribution to discussions with students and supervisors after being interviewed as in providing a measure of learning style. Although Pask reports students as having a characteristic approach to learning, which will be reflected in their approach to the Clobbits exercise, it seems more likely that strategies used will only be characteristic for those with a relatively simple, fixed, conception of learning. Pask's report that those who had used holist strategies were more easily induced to use serialist strategies in subsequent exercises seems to confirm this.

It also became clear that match or mis-match between the approaches of teachers and learners in the exercise need not produce difficulties in supervision, since one or both might be versatile in their learning strategies.

Whilst more subjects adopted holist than serialist strategies, other approaches were identified. One subject looked at all the cards from A1, A2 . . . successively through to E5 because he thought that was what he ought to do, since they were numbered and lettered in order. (This supervisor, and a placement he was involved in, are the first case illustration in Chapter 6). Two versions of a random strategy were found: one was where entirely random cards were selected to build up the taxonomy; the other was the use of a randomized strategy at first, to sample the kinds of information available in each group, before moving on to more focused (and holist) strategies.

One person refused outright to do the exercise during the period of the study. Having had threequarters of an hour reading the material and not establishing what she was meant to do, she wrote on her response sheet 'Winston Smith started his diary on 4th April 1984. I think I now know why!'. This reference to the book *Nineteen Eighty-Four* (Orwell 1945) was not only literally accurate but was written on the exact day described in the book (she was indeed being asked to do the exercise on 4 April 1984!).

The rest of the major data collection phase of the study is reported in the next two chapters (including some individual findings from the learning styles exercise). It was predominantly a phase of tape-recorded interviews, together with following up of relevant other material. The development of the approach is described first, with case illustrations following.

5

The Anatomy of Supervision:
A Case Example

5.1 The development of the case example approach

In the earlier phase of data collection, it had not been possible to clarify or debate the responses to the questionnaire nor to discuss the taped material in the single case study. This pointed to the need to interview as a prime method of data collection. Because teaching and learning processes are interactive, and could change through time, it was decided to focus on whole placements, through taped interviews with both students and supervisors.

This approach would give an opportunity to address issues of match and mis-match of learning styles and stages which might have affected events during the placement. The need to gather data in depth, and to include the interpretations placed on events by the participants, would constrain the number of placements to be covered. However, in both Perry's (1970) and Laurillard's (1978) research valuable results were demonstrated with quite small samples. It was decided therefore to try to gather data from about twelve to fifteen pairs of students and supervisors, and to produce case examples to illustrate the kinds of data found.

The usefulness of the findings of the earlier single case study derived from the quality and depth of the material. The value of the questionnaire exercise came from the range of responses to general questions about teaching and learning as they related to the supervisor's own experience. The focus in this stage was to gather material in less depth and detail than tape-recording the supervision sessions from an entire placement, but to provide the opportunity to explore further the issues raised, and to begin to interpret that material.

The single case study had been selected on the basis of being not untypical, and avoiding extreme or unusual characteristics of student, supervisor and the context in which the placement took place. Here, the range of placements was decided upon by ensuring coverage, by types of CQSW courses, and by spreading the gathering of data throughout the United Kingdom. There was no explicit attempt to randomize the selection, nor to seek representative cases.

Some supervisors who had completed questionnaires earlier were followed up. All of the students were previously unknown to the researcher.

There is a bias, therefore, towards more experienced supervisors, although two were chosen because they were supervising an assessed placement for the first time. It is possible that a large range of supervisors has been excluded, but the response to the case illustrations, which have been shown to participants and others in social work education, suggests that they succeed in depicting recognizable realities, and do not seem to have overlooked whole classes of supervisors. If the classical supervision model is widespread, then we might expect to find examples of its influence (and, possibly) the problems it may cause, in almost any sample if it is widely drawn along certain dimensions.

The interviews were therefore carried out over a period of eighteen months throughout the United Kingdom. About half were carried out in London and the Home Counties; smaller numbers of interviews were undertaken elsewhere in England, in the Highlands of Scotland, and in Northern Ireland. Placements from post-graduate, non-graduate and 4-year degree courses were included, although there was no attempt to ensure equal (or proportionate) numbers from each kind of course. Courses in universities and polytechnics were covered. The gender balance of students reflected the general ratio of three female to two male, but no black students were picked up, even though about nine per cent of course intakes of that period were students from ethnic minority groups (Gardiner 1985). One physically handicapped student was included in the sample.

A later development was to take account of the CCETSW review of its qualifying training policies and foreshadow developments in the future patterns of social work education by including some interviews with Certificate of Social Service (CSS) students and supervisors from schemes where there were practice placements.

The pattern adopted was to interview either the supervisor or the student whilst the other person completed the learning styles (Clobbits) exercise, then the roles were reversed. At first, there was not a planned order in the interviews, but after a few had been completed, encouragement was given to the supervisor to be interviewed first, because the interviews with supervisors gave more of the context and background to the placement.

In all of the interviews in this part of the study, the chance to talk together as a threesome after the formal part of the interviews, was offered. Usually this was done by saying 'I should like to offer some feedback on how you completed the learning styles exercise, and to comment on any connections between it and the teaching and learning processes on the placement which had emerged in the interviews'. It became obvious that this opportunity triggered, for students and their supervisors, the making of important connections between elements of learning, and events on the placement. Therefore, these sessions were also tape-recorded. They generated some of the most important material of all that was collected in this phase. They were also a major contribution to checking the accuracy of data and interpretations.

In these interviews, there was not a laid-down, pre-planned schedule but a clear and consistent pattern evolved: they began with a sketch of the main purpose of the research as 'trying to focus attention on teaching and learning during the placement' and that the researcher 'was interested in the processes of *how* people taught and learned as well as at *what* was taught and learned'. It was usually suggested to the supervisors that they began by talking about the decision to have this student on placement, and to continue chronologically from there. To the students, it was suggested that they talked about the first meeting with this supervisor, and/or from when they knew that this was to be their placement.

The approach seemed a useful device since it allowed both supervisor and student to develop their own stories of the placement from its inception. They did not always attach the same weight to events, although on most occasions they were largely agreed on the major issues, episodes and experiences. In listening to the tapes subsequently, the readiness and openness with which the overwhelming majority talked, and the lengths to which they went to be helpful in describing their own experiences of the placement, is striking.

In addition to studying some placements as case examples, the data concerning those individuals from throughout the study are reported here as Case Illustrations. Case studies have been recognized as a particularly appropriate way of undertaking qualitative educational research (MacDonald and Walker 1977):

> . . . where there are problems of the researcher-practitioner relationship . . . where there are institutionalised mythologies designed to protect participants from the public gaze . . . Education has generated a reflective language which has theoretical, analytic and descriptive concepts which allow the case study to be presented in the language of those being studied . . .
> . . . case studies are selective in choice of focus and way of synthesising data by case rather than by issues . . . the single instance approach of the artist leading to an attempt to present universals through a unique image has to be fused with the need to reflect commonalities and similarities . . .

Certainly, this study is attempting to develop 'a reflective language which has theoretical, analytic and descriptive concepts which allow the case study to be presented in the language of those being studied'. Supervision is rarely open to view, and this was stressed in an early report of the study (Gardiner, 1984b). In response, Badger (1985a) has commented:

> As Gardiner himself points out, 'supervision is a very private experience' and contributing, as it does, the major element in practice assessment, is long overdue for detailed research.

MacDonald and Walker's second point helps the consideration of whether to represent the data gathered at a level of generality to look for commonalities encompassing all, or most, of the placements studied; or whether to search for a single case to represent them all. A middle road was chosen, with key examples presented at considerable length, and some others in less detail.

Patton (1978) has also discussed the merits of case approaches, in the general context of offering a range of models which combine ways of collecting and representing qualitative data. Perhaps the most important argument here in favour is the contribution of the case approach to model-building and to theory-building. Not only are actual cases described and presented, but they can be the basis of grounded theory (Glaser and Strauss 1967).

The case examples reported in the next two chapters not only represent the range of data collected, but also contribute to the building of an interactive model of teaching and learning in professional education.

5.2   Case illustration I – a successful placement

This placement is one of the earliest included in this phase of the study. A number of general points about it help to set the scene. In some ways it is a typical placement: it is the final placement on a two-year, non-graduate CQSW course in the maintained sector. It takes place in the area team office in a large county social services department about thirty miles from the educational institution.

The student had substantial experience of social work, prior to beginning the course, in a nearby authority. He is a graduate in psychology, but did not choose to go to a course for graduates. *The supervisor* is supervising her first professional placement, having previously taken students for observation placements. She had only completed sheet one in the questionnaire exercise, since she had at that time not supervised an assessed placement. She was invited to be involved in the research because of her interest in social work education, and because it was the first assessed placement she had supervised. She was included to balance up rather more experienced supervisors in the sample.

The interviews were carried out on the day after the placement finished, and are (in comparison with all interviews carried out during the course of the study) two of the most coherent; they required little intervention in the form of direct questioning or prompting by the interviewer. They also were amongst the most satisfying to carry out. This case illustration includes the first taped feedback session, following the individual interviews with the student and supervisor. Some of the material included is very personal, so I am grateful to these two participants in particular for allowing the material to be used.

These interviews are reported in considerable detail for a number of reasons: first, they illustrate within a single placement many of the features of the teaching and learning processes which emerged in this main phase of data collection. Consequently it is useful to present this case study in detail, before presenting others.

Second, the clear evidence of movement and change during the placement allows the development of conceptualizations about stages, as well as styles, of teaching and learning – so it makes a considerable contribution to model-building. Third, it gives a clear indication of the role and contribution of the researcher to the interviews, and allows critical examination of his involvement. It was indicated above that in qualitative research it is essential that the methods of collecting data, and the influence of the interviewer, as well as possible bias in selection of materials, need to be addressed in this way. A fourth reason is the clear and explicit way these participants described events, their patterns of interaction, and the meanings they attached at the time (and subsequently) to their experiences.

Finally, it allows others to consider the raw data, and offer different interpretations and conceptualizations. The almost total absence of such material, in detailed accounts, from the supervision literature is a powerful argument for including it here in such detail.

The interviews are reported without comment first, and are followed by a commentary section. In looking at them, it is important to note data which illumine the kinds of issues already identified:

the ways in which student and supervisor see the learning task;

the approaches to teaching and learning which they use;

the *impact of differences in approach* between student and supervisor;

indications of change and development for learner or teacher, and consequent *changes in the pattern of their interaction* through the placement;

the *impact of assessment* on teacher and learner behaviour, and their interactions.

5.2.1 The interview with the student

As in all reports of interviews in this chapter, quotations are from the student, or supervisor, except those indicated by (*Interviewer*). All names and places which could identify those involved have been excluded. Additions in parentheses are included to maintain the sense where intervening material has been left out. Hesitations and repetitions are generally excluded, though they are reported where they seem to be important.

[After an introduction about the focus and purpose of the research, with the intention to look at teaching and learning processes, the student was asked to begin by describing his expectations of the placement. There had been a College form to complete, for spelling out placement needs, to which his replies were 'broad, vague and mechanistic . . . I wasn't encouraged to think it out . . . I left it to the last minute . . . If I am not going to be glib, I need someone to lead me into sophistication and subtlety . . . I didn't do this exercise very well . . .']

. . . [at the first meeting with the supervisor, in college] she'd take something I said simplistically . . . she'd say 'What do you mean by that?'

and lead me down avenues to specific behavioural statements . . . the scene was set for specificity and explicitness . . . At the pre-placement visit to discuss the contract skeleton, we had to fill in the five sections: Knowledge to be learned; Skills to be learned; Linking theory and practice; Work to be undertaken; Other . . .'

(*Interviewer*) Looking back . . . *how* did you think you were going to learn these things? . . .

I passed it [responsibility] over to my supervisor. Now I'd be in a better position to talk about how I'd see myself learning . . . I'd give it a lot more thought . . . not glib, at the last minute . . . (there was discussion about going back to work at the end of the course) . . . I have got a meeting planned with this supervisor, my new supervisor and my college tutor . . .

(*Interviewer*) When you first started, what was it like?

It was like starting a new job . . . simple skills like learning to use the telephone, and who the bosses were . . . My supervisor thought I should be doing other things, and learning to use the telephone would come . . . I started by doing visits of observation to other agencies in the locality to see the philosophy of the district I was in . . .

There was a bit of a clash there . . . I was resistant . . . I'd been a social worker for three years . . . and done two other social services placements . . . I suppose I saw them all [services] as being similar . . . [but now he says he is planning to do just this when he gets back from his course and starts work in a new area] . . .

I did it because I was the student and she was the supervisor . . . that was another of the changes . . . students do what supervisors say, if they're sensible . . . If I had another placement, I'd now feel more confident, to speak my individual mind, rather than just go along with what the superior person is saying . . .

The power relationship was the thing, almost an obsession . . . we talked at very great length about her power . . . the pass-fail power . . . I thought if she says 'do placement visits', and if I want to pass, I do placement visits . . . My present supervisor has helped me to change in myself – I won't be a passive employee or passive student in future . . .

(*Interviewer*) How has that come about?

. . . My supervisor said, just the other day, she had the power over pass-fail, but I had the power to achieve it [the necessary performance] . . . I hadn't grasped that . . . I mean trust is there, about the not unreasonable use of power . . .

My other fieldwork supervisor did not want to talk me out of that frame of mind, that I did not have power. He was quite happy that I should think that . . . whereas my present placement supervisor said that up front . . . and said it was a bar to my development . . . and retrospectively she was wise in doing that . . .

(*Interviewer*) . . . how did you get this confidence, to move from this passive, responsive student kind of position, to having more responsibility?

Yesterday in the three-way [a discussion between him, his tutor and the supervisor] she [the tutor] says 'It's a riddle with him, he can do this, this and this, but at the same time he's quite passive. . . . He didn't have practice knowledge, it only really developed in this placement' . . . but now it's different, out of this placement I have confidence in my competence . . . it's quite a nice feeling . . .

We sorted that out at quite a late stage [in the placement] . . . it was there, in the contract, we mentioned the 'lack of confidence' in the previous supervisor's report [of the earlier placement] . . . it was really a lack of competence . . . we had to work that one out.

I'd take the risks that I knew I could handle, but I've been encouraged by my supervisor to do that – previously there was no support for techniques that weren't agency policy.

(*Interviewer*) This supervisor gave you more space and support than the previous supervisor. How do you think she was doing this?

God moves in mysterious ways! . . . the [present] agency was more tolerant, but [the supervisor] was dogmatic about the family approach so she'd encourage any students in that way . . . other people in the office weren't hostile . . . in my previous agencies they might well be . . . if they saw a student doing something special they are not able to do.

(*Interviewer*) . . . and the supervisor, did she have a part in this?

My ongoing assessment of her was that she appeared to be a competent social worker . . . [which] was important to me, to command my respect . . . we really confined consultation to supervision sessions, weekly for two hours or so. We'd look at a case in detail, she would suggest, or provide a range of courses of action, and leave me to select [one] and then go away and get on with it . . . she was providing pretty general sorts of strategies . . .

If I took one up she'd give me more details . . . an example of that would be a sculpting [he described an incident with a family, after which he had got stuck] . . . after I'd done it I didn't know what to do next . . .

(*Interviewer*) She wasn't prescriptive, but allowed choice, and then she offered specific technical help and support?

Yes, and she'd present it in an acceptable way . . . if she'd been *telling* me what to do it wouldn't have worked . . . she'd probably got me sussed out quite well . . .

(*Interviewer*) Implied in that is that she'd got some idea of where you were at, as a learner . . . How do you think she'd done that?

One had the impression she was one step ahead of me in trying to understand my future needs, she'd be prepared for what I'd bring next time . . .

(*Interviewer*) How do you think she managed that?

How she made that assessment, mmmm . . . that would be a mystery to me . . . I don't really know, I couldn't begin to imagine . . . [The interviewer started to prompt, to ask this again in a different way, but the student carried on.] No, I've had an idea, I think her own learning experience would be relevant . . . she would not give definite illustrations – she'd convey a pattern from her own learning . . . I don't think [the supervisor] and I would say that this model was the correct one for [all] supervision. I would imagine it was how she was trained herself . . .

(*Interviewer*) What things have you learnt on the placement, or the single most important thing, about yourself?

I've learnt confidence in my competence . . . [he pauses]

(*Interviewer*) How might I know that, if I were watching you practise?

. . . from the quality of my assessments, and actions I was taking on them . . . preparedness to reassess . . . [my intervention] was sharper at each stage of the process, and had a qualitative difference . . . the systems approach, and the family therapy option is now a whole new possibility in my cases . . .

I've also discovered 'humanity' in my work, to bring in sensitivity and empathy in my work.

(*Interviewer*) Can you tell me a bit more about this, about *how* this happened?

There was a death in the office . . . [one of the social workers, who had been ill] she was a friend of my supervisor . . . it was quite a shock to the whole office. That experience made me human in my dealings with my clients . . . I became a different sort of worker . . . and my supervisor, this high up, superior, person with powers of pass-fail, she became human herself – she was upset, vulnerable – as did the whole office . . . I carved out a [special] role . . . in assisting these people with their grief . . .

(*Interviewer*) So you could give up being the office-student, the learner, and junior, you could also be a provider?

Yes, the release from that role . . . it improved my confidence and individual standing, I was not just the office-student . . . It was facilitated by the selection of my cases [around this time], they weren't just cases every student gets . . .

(*Interviewer*) So you weren't just the student, you could be different . . . and use your abilities as a person, [you had them] in your other life, but now you could bring them into your work, and it was OK to do that . . .

I wasn't like that previously, in my work I mean . . . they didn't expect you to be like that in [where he worked before coming onto the course].

(*Interviewer*) So you could give up being adult, and traditionally male, as well as being a student, and be vulnerable and caring?

Yes . . . [he describes how he is like that at home, but had not before thought that it could be part of his professional role].

(*Interviewer*) Do you think that things were already changing, a bit, and [the colleague's] death just crystallized it out . . . I mean do you think it would have happened anyway, perhaps not quite so quickly? . . . Couldn't it have happened anyway, with a different kind of challenge?

[There is an exchange about how other crises bring about change for different kinds of students.]
   . . . I suppose I was at the mechanistic end of the continuum . . . this was the kick I needed . . . this sort of thing was never made clear by myself or my previous supervisors or my tutor, to my present supervisor, that I was this sort of person.

(*Interviewer*) [after a summary of the last exchanges] . . . I suppose that this shift had quite an impact on supervision, too?

Generally it facilitated it. I started to look at the power thing differently. I had some power of my own, too. I could use it in a caring way . . . I could use supervision as less of a management exercise . . . My supervisor would have had it that way all along and it was me who wanted it to be a management exercise . . . clear cut, mechanistic, and at the right end of the continuum . . .
   The thing about the death, as a crystallization, it only emerged yesterday, in the three-way, our final three-way meeting [between student, tutor and supervisor] . . . was when it publically emerged as a root of change.

(*Interviewer*) Yes, maybe it's only with hindsight we can see the significance of those things . . . In summary, you've made significant progress, not just in the way you might have predicted?

There's no way I could have predicted this. I was like a pioneer, an adventurer, [but] . . . I couldn't shape the adventuring journey to my needs. I was delegating that to somebody else. I don't think I'll do that again in the future . . .

(*Interviewer*) I had about fifty students, as a supervisor, and I think that, I remember with most of my students, and in my own course . . . I think it is pretty common, this shift in how you see yourself, in your professional role . . . of course, it doesn't always happen so dramatically . . . I remember that kind of shift with others, from trying out professional, technical-type skills, and realizing that they didn't have to contain their feelings, their experience all the time, but could make use of it . . .

Did you find there were there things, that were the equivalent, to a death
. . . you can get that out of a case situation as well?

(*Interviewer*) Yes, sometimes a case; sometimes I think students were going
through a very important crisis themselves . . . or a crisis with one of the
other students in the group, like when someone leaves, or there was a failing
student in the Unit . . . things like that often seemed to bring about a
crystallization for others . . . yes, or sometimes it was a crisis in the
supervision relationship itself . . .

. . . I wanted to use the word *paradigm* yesterday, in the report, but it wasn't
a permissible word, so it wasn't included.

(*Interviewer*) A shift of paradigm, in how you operate, and see yourself as a
worker? ['Yes.'] I think that's a really good way of summing it up.

[The student is thanked for his involvement and the interview ends.]

At the beginning of this interview, the student describes his approach to the
placement, and emphasizes that he did not feel that he was very good at
specifying his own learning needs, nor at taking the initiative in relation to his
own learning. He saw that as the responsibility of his supervisor:

> . . . I wasn't encouraged to think it out . . . I left it to the last minute . . . If I
> am not going to be glib, I need someone to lead me into sophistication and
> subtlety . . .
> I passed it [responsibility] over to my supervisor. Now I'd be in a better
> position to talk about how I'd see myself learning . . . I'd give it a lot more
> thought . . . not glib, at the last minute . . .

The student acknowledges that even when he did think about things, early in
the placement, he still saw the supervisor as being in authority, and her power to
pass or fail him meant that he decided to fit in with her requirements:

> There was a bit of a clash there . . . I was resistant . . . I'd been a social
> worker for three years . . . I did it because I was the student and she was the
> supervisor . . . students do what supervisors say, if they're sensible . . .
> The power relationship was the thing, almost an obsession . . . we talked
> at very great length about her power . . . the pass-fail power . . . I thought if
> she says 'do placement visits', and if I want to pass, I do placement
> visits . . .

However, the student later shows that things are somewhat different now, and
in a similar situation, he would act more assertively:

> If I had another placement, I'd now feel more confident, to speak my
> individual mind, rather than just go along with what the superior person is
> saying . . .
> My present supervisor has helped me to change in myself – I won't be a
> passive employee or passive student in future . . .

This change is due to increased confidence, which has come in part from being able to take risks in new ways of working, and from feeling that his supervisor would support him:

I'd take the risks that I knew I could handle, but I've been encouraged by my supervisor to do that . . .

The student believes in the supervisor, and trusts her judgement, because she is a competent professional; but he also responds to the fact that she presents him with a range of possible actions, and allows him the choice:

My ongoing assessment of her was that she appeared to be a competent social worker . . . [which] was important to me, to command my respect . . . We'd look at a case in detail, she would suggest, or provide a range of courses of action, and leave me to select [one] and then go away and get on with it . . . she was providing pretty general sorts of strategies . . . If I took one up she'd give me more details . . . and she'd present it in an acceptable way . . . if she'd been *telling* me what to do it wouldn't have worked . . . she'd probably got me sussed out quite well . . .

This is very different from the way the supervisor in the single case study earlier had approached how to intervene in a case:

The first discussion of a particular case the student was taking on included the supervisor saying 'I don't think there will be anything to sort out . . . it's probably a question of making arrangements to meet people . . . and I suggest making an appointment to see the school counsellor . . .'

That supervisor had told the student exactly who to contact, and had gone on to rehearse him in the right way to do things.

The student here goes on to describe how his supervisor has encouraged and allowed him to develop a wider range of interventive approaches than he was previously competent to offer:

My [intervention] was sharper at each stage of the process, and had a qualitative difference . . . the systems approach, and the family therapy option is now a whole new possibility in my cases . . .

The student says he saw the supervisor as having expertise not only as a practitioner, but also as a teacher, and begins to articulate this by first stating the position he adopted at the beginning of the placement – but then making some connections for the first time, during the interview itself:

One had the impression she was one step ahead of me in trying to understand my future needs, she'd be prepared for what I'd bring next time . . . How she made that I couldn't begin to imagine . . . No, I've had an idea, I think her own learning experience would be relevant . . . she would not give definite illustrations – she'd convey a pattern from her own learning . . . I would imagine it was how she was trained herself . . .

The student goes on to describe the crisis in the office following the death of one of the team, and its impact on him in his relationship with his supervisor; and then, crucially, in his work as well:

> I've also discovered 'humanity' in my work, to bring in sensitivity and empathy in my work . . . There was a death in the office . . . it was quite a shock to the whole office. That experience made me human in my dealings with my clients . . . I became a different sort of worker . . . and my supervisor, this high up, superior, pass-fail person with powers of pass-fail, she became human herself – she was upset, vulnerable – as did the whole office . . . I carved out a [special] role . . . in assisting these people with their grief . . . I wasn't like that previously, in my work I mean . . . they didn't expect you to be like that in [where he worked before coming onto the course].

The student here is giving up his earlier ideas that there might be a single right way to practise social work, to which he should aspire if he wishes to pass; and that his supervisor is someone with special powers and abilities (derived from her authority and expertise). Instead, he begins to recognize the importance of involving and using himself in his work, and not operating as an objective, detached professional. The pattern of supervision is also different as a result of these changes, with the student realizing that his own learning is a personal journey, and that he had to make it on his own:

> Generally it facilitated it. I started to look at the power thing differently. I had some power of my own, too. I could use it in a caring way . . . I could use supervision as less of a management exercise . . . My supervisor would have had it that way all along and it was me who wanted it to be a management exercise . . . There's no way I could have predicted this. I was like a pioneer, an adventurer, [but] . . . I couldn't shape the adventuring journey to my needs. I was delegating that to somebody else. I don't think I'll do that again in the future . . .

There is then a part of the interview where the interviewer responds to the importance of the material he has just heard, helping the student to frame some of his experience on this placement by generalizing, and indicating that although the death was a powerful precipitating factor, the kinds of changes (in practice and supervision) which the student describes are by no means unusual during placements:

> (*Interviewer*) I think it is pretty common, this shift in how you see yourself, in your professional role . . . I remember that kind of shift with others, from trying out professional, technical-type skills, and realizing that they didn't have to contain their feelings, their experience all the time, but could make use of it . . . [it was] sometimes a case; sometimes I think students were going through a very important crisis themselves . . . or a crisis with one of the other students in the group, like when someone leaves, or there was a failing student in the Unit . . . things like that often seemed to bring about a crystallization for others . . . yes, or sometimes it was a crisis in the supervision relationship itself . . .

The student sums up by explaining how his understanding of these experiences was made clearer, and explicit, during a joint discussion with tutor and supervisor the previous day, and that this has fundamentally changed how he sees himself, and his experiences on the placement. Many of the themes here recur in other interviews, and are resonant with the researcher's own experiences as a supervisor. These themes and issues are developed later, after a detailed account of the interview with the supervisor.

5.2.2 *Interview with the supervisor*

The supervisor qualified as a social worker four years before the beginning of this placement, and has worked as an area team social worker dealing with predominantly statutory child care cases for the past two years. She has attended workshops and conferences on supervision, but has not previously supervised an assessed placement.

[There was the usual introduction by the researcher about the focus of the study on teaching and learning, including the distinction between *what* and *how* things are taught and learnt. The supervisor was invited to talk about the placement chronologically.]

It was to be his final placement, and he'd had three years experience before the course, and other non-social work experience in the local authority . . . his previous placements had also been in social services . . . it seemed to me at that point he'd had a heavy overdose of social services . . . I wanted to establish what his own goals were for this placement . . . he didn't seem to have very clear ideas [about them] . . . he seemed quite reluctant to make definite statements . . . At that point I wasn't sure whether he didn't have any ideas (and that was how it was coming across to me) . . . or whether for some reason he wasn't able to say . . .

(*Interviewer*) So what did you do about that?

I guess I started to talk to him about his previous experience, to get some understanding of the level at which he was, at that point in time, so I could get a kind of picture of the stage he was, when he was beginning his placement . . . and I married that up with my own expectations of where I thought he should have been . . . [and] where he should be at the end of the placement, and tried to discuss these with [him] and his tutor . . . Basically it seemed like everything was rather hazy, neither [he] nor his tutor had very clear ideas as to what it was that he was wanting to achieve in a final placement. [He] was very conscious of going back into social services, so he wanted to be proficient as a social worker in social services, and have a very sound knowledge of practice in social services that would equip him for when he went back to [his seconding agency].

(*Interviewer*) So you moved on to a placement contract . . . can you remember . . . *how* you thought you would try to meet some of those things that were in the contract . . . you must have had, kind of, a sense of *how* he was going to do that learning?

I had my own expectations, though they weren't married very closely with [the student's] expectations, nor his tutor's. Their side of it all seemed very hazy to me. I took a much more assertive role in laying out what I expected he should do . . . then [he] began to discuss that. I posed the framework . . . [and we] arrived at a mutual agreement . . . I felt that [he] didn't have any notion of the social work process, and that was one area in the contract . . . to work on the integration of theory and practice to do with the social work process . . . in a thorough and systematic way from when he first received the referral . . . It was quite structured, but it was necessary for me to get some gauge of [his] ability, to get some sort of baseline for myself to know where he was . . . I also had a lot of anxieties about his actual level of competence, and therefore felt that I needed to be very involved as a supervisor, and probably if necessary quite directive.

At the beginning of the placement I was extremely directive, and stated very clearly what my expectations were, and from that basis [we] began to discuss things . . . there were some things which he felt would offer him nothing in terms of a learning experience.

(*Interviewer*) Do you remember what those things were?

Specifically, I felt that it was important as a new person to visit different agencies in the area, for one reason to see how they worked in our area, and two, to meet the various people he would be working with on this placement. [He] felt that this was a real waste of his time, because he had worked in social services for years and years, and thought he knew how other agencies worked, and didn't see any value in having personal contact . . .

I felt strongly that he should do that . . . so we agreed he would try it out and reassess, after a period of trial whether it was valuable . . . He decided himself it was valuable for him . . . I was very strong at the beginning that he must make a point of reading the theory to do with the social work process, and we talked a lot [about it] in supervision, trying to integrate it in a theoretical way, and then started that process with his clients . . . we discussed, very fully, each case and I structured his thinking about each stage [of the social work process].

(*Interviewer*) How did he respond to that degree of structure, or 'directiveness' was the word you used?

I think in some ways he really resented it, and felt that I was treating him at a lesser level than he felt himself [to be] . . . and at the same time, because we had a contract [about this kind of work] and we discussed various ways of how to do it, and the possible outcome, and then we both came to a decision about how he would go about it. We didn't have any confrontations . . . but he felt that I had the power even if he'd wanted to rebel. He wanted to learn, as well . . . so he acquiesced . . . to try out what I was suggesting – on the basis that we would try it, and if it wasn't working, we would look at it again and do something else. I think that arose because [he] didn't come up with any other ideas . . . so I took the initiative.

(*Interviewer*) So it would be fair to say that in that early part of the placement, the way that the teacher and learner interacted was that you were pretty directive, and he was pretty passive? ['Yes'] Was that a pattern that stayed, throughout the placement?

No, no. I think it changed a lot . . . [he] increasingly became motivated to seek out his own learning, and became much more imaginative and creative in terms of his work . . . he was always very keen to follow up the literature . . . no-one had ever encouraged him to do that in the past . . . and that snowballed, as the placement went on, he took much more responsibility for initiating his own learning, and I think my role changed quite markedly.

(*Interviewer*) How would you describe it then, towards the end [of the placement]?

Basically, at the end of the placement [he] made the decisions about how he was going to work, what he was going to do, and I encouraged him and supported him in what he was doing . . . if he had areas of difficulty, we discussed those in depth . . . [how he could use] different ways of resolving a problem . . . so the relationship became much more balanced.

(*Interviewer*) Can you remember, in terms of your assessment of his competence, when the change came about, from the beginning when you had said he was vague and woolly, and you had some doubts about his competence, and the end when you'd passed him . . . when did that change take place? Did it occur gradually, over a long time, or were there some significant turning points? Was there a point when you thought he was a passing student, not a possible failing student?

We had a midway assessment . . . and about two or three weeks prior to that I had decided his practice was up to passing level. At the midpoint assessment, in a meeting with his tutor, it was made quite clear that if [he] continued [like that] . . . he would pass the placement.

(*Interviewer*) Did that seem to affect how he related to you as well?

I don't think it was at the midpoint assessment . . . [he] and I had discussed it . . . it happened earlier, and may have been related to er, I don't know. [Pause] Coming at it the other way, early on in the placement, we had a discussion about trust. [He] said he found it difficult to put trust in me . . . [because of the power to fail him] but he made a conscious decision, we made an agreement . . . to try it out . . . That seemed to be a critical turning point, fairly early on, in the first month . . . From that point on, as far as I was concerned, the whole thing seemed to improve . . . I had the power to fail him, and that seemed to be a blocking mechanism.

(*Interviewer*) [Restates this] . . . and this was prior to you feeling he was going to pass – was that in a way the opportunity for him to go out and demonstrate in his practice what gave you the assurance that he was going to pass?

Yes, I think that's absolutely right.

(*Interviewer*) They were two quite distinct stages: one was the element of trust in the stage when you were the powerful authority figure, and he was the passive, student figure. ['Yes'] And then that led to something happening in his practice that reassured you about his level of performance in his practice?

Yes, that's exactly right, and one of the things we built into our contract was that [he] wanted regular feedback, and I was very conscious, right from the word go, to give him continuous feedback, both positive and negative . . . Anything that was done well I would praise, and things that I was critical of, I would criticize. That was an ongoing feature, right throughout the placement . . . [He] did not want to reach the end of the placement without knowing [if he was going to pass] . . . I was very conscious of praising for things done well, not just being critical . . . Then he made the leap of faith, the conscious decision to trust me.

(*Interviewer*) Later in the placement, the pattern was obviously very different. How would you describe the pattern?

Can you be more specific?

(*Interviewer*) [Restates, and adds] . . . earlier, you used words like 'acquiescent', but at the end of the placement it wasn't like that . . . how was it, if it wasn't like that?

[She describes three areas of his work, with illustrations]. He, with little guidance from me after planning the initial contact, planning the first visit . . . he made a plan which we discussed in supervision, and after that point he basically did his own planning and intervention . . . My role in supervision was mainly to praise what he had done, to encourage him, to broaden out what he had done and put what he had done into a more rounded picture . . . if he came to any areas where he was stuck, we would discuss those.

(*Interviewer*) Could you give me an example of one of those . . . and how you responded to that? [Pause] Can I prompt you with an incident [he] talked about in his interview? [The interviewer gives details of the family sculpting exercise.]

We then talked about the use of sculpting in general terms, and what had happened in this family, and I broadened out what he thought had happened into a more theoretical context, because his theory wasn't sufficiently developed . . . and planned . . . [how he could use what he had done] on his next visit.

(*Interviewer*) I can understand him being more explicit, and more focused, but were there other qualitative differences in his work, between your initial fears, and what was happening at the end . . . ?

By being very pedantic about the social work process, and stressing the importance of . . . [more structured] work gave him more direction in his work with his clients . . . That enabled him to have a basic framework from which he could be more creative and imaginative . . .

(*Interviewer*) Could you give me an example of that?

One of the things that really struck me, it was a quite simple thing, but a very important thing, was that one of his elderly men clients decided, after a great deal of discussion, and after being in Part Three [accommodation] for a holiday, to go in on a permanent basis. [The student] offered to help, and talked to him about the furniture and personal belongings he would like to take with him. One of the very important things he wanted to take was his own bed. [The student] measured the bed, and then measured up the room, to check it would fit. Then he planned with this man that he would take the bed on his car, he would transport the man and his bed together to the home, which was [the student's] way of signifying the importance of everybody going together, and his belongings were going with them. I thought that was a very thoughtful incident which illustrated the personal qualities which he could bring into his work. There were similar incidents with families . . . [which she recounted.]

(*Interviewer*) They are good examples during the placement of shifts in his work with clients, but what about shifts in supervision, and in his relationship with you?

We went through that time of him trusting me, and following my instructions as it were, and then came another critical point, when my colleague [in the office] died. The whole office were extremely grief stricken about that . . . There were implications on several levels. One was that I didn't have the time, or the personal energy, to offer him anything much outside of supervision. The only time I saw him was during the supervision sessions, but even during that time, I didn't feel I was operating at my proper capacity, I was so preoccupied with my own grief. I felt I was almost like a client in a sense, because I was needing to be taken care of. I wasn't able to give him the time I would have liked, nor to give him anything extra. He was thrown onto his own devices. The whole atmosphere was of grief and sadness for at least a month. I was different, the whole office was different. He was very kind to me in terms of not making demands on me, and doing thoughtful things . . . and only asking me things if it was vital. I think that at the end of that time things had changed quite dramatically for both of us.

That is something we talked about in the final three-way meeting [with the tutor] yesterday. It was something we had not been able to make explicit until that point in time . . .

(*Interviewer*) Can you say a bit about the way it did affect him, and his role?

. . . Because of my extreme grief, and that of my colleagues . . . we were an office full of people grieving, rather than an office full of social workers . . . [he] saw me in this state of grief, and saw me so upset, that's when he changed, and responded to me on a human level, as anyone would with someone who was in grief rather than as his supervisor . . .

Because people were so open in the office, with their feelings, with their grief, that was transferred onto his work with clients, working on a higher emotional level . . . he really thought about how the clients were feeling . . . he introduced humanity into his work, rather than working by the book . . . it felt comfortable, and easier for him, and he has retained [this] . . . [He] thinks it has dramatically enabled him to increase his competence in practice, and to relate to me on a different basis.

(*Interviewer*) . . . that came after his decision to trust you, but before you'd decided he'd pass?

I didn't realize it at the time . . . but in retrospect it was obviously very significant, yes. I thought at the time it was because he had been freed to get on with his own work . . . and he'd responded well to that independence . . .

(*Interviewer*) . . . things had started before, but had crystallized out around that time? ['Yes'] is it likely that things would have crystallized out, if there had not been that crisis in the office?

. . . [yes] it would seem that the same kinds of things would have happened, from what [he] said, but not at that pace . . . his rate of progress would have been more constant, not exponential growth . . . [he] is the kind of person who needs a crisis to respond to, otherwise he tries to play it safe . . .

(*Interviewer*) Is that how he was when he came . . . ?

Yes, he wanted very much to pass the placement . . . he would do what was right, in order to pass. By his own admission, he had been doing that throughout the entire course . . . Having a contract gave him a target, it was a kind of mini-crisis, he'd never had one before . . . he was really anxious that he wouldn't pass . . .

(*Interviewer*) Were there any parallels between how he learnt on his placement, and how you learnt on yours . . . ?

I think I taught him in a very similar way to how I had been taught by my supervisor, and my expectations, both of him and myself, were based on me as a student. I think at the end of the placement there were a lot of similarities between how [he] and I learnt, but at the beginning we were quite different. I trusted my supervisors implicitly, and I didn't have a paranoia about passing . . .

[He] has been enabled to state his own attitudes now, and they seem similar to mine, but at the beginning, he was saying what he thought would be a good thing to say and what would get him through . . . We both work best from a structured framework, we both need the theoretical input as well as the practice, and are able to integrate the two . . . a little bit of practice, then a little bit of theory . . .

(*Interviewer*) Is there anything else, that we haven't covered?

Only that he used other people in my office, that I wasn't the only person . . . he made use of, and was used by, others in our Department. [She gave an example relating to the new Mental Health Act.]

(*Interviewer*) Can you say how it came about?

At the beginning it was decided that he would do some work with elderly clients, and I didn't have any [clients, and expertise] . . . I suggested others in the office had a lot of experience and it would be better to discuss with them. That's a common theme running right through, I'd point something out, he was motivated to try it out . . . the team were helpful, but people felt he'd given as much as he'd gained, it was two way.

Other significant things included the involvement of the tutor . . . new things always came out in the three-way meetings . . .

(*Interviewer*) In rounding things off . . . I'd like to say something of the importance of the use people make of crises . . . we can never protect people from them, nor structure them in. What strikes me very much from the discussions with each of you was how hard both of you had worked to make use of the experiences . . . on the placement . . . [and that is why so much came out of it.]

Sure, I think that's absolutely right . . . we're both determined and work hard and have the stamina to see things through right to the very end.

(*Interviewer*) That's probably a good point to end on . . . thank you very much.

This interview is notable for the clear and articulate way the supervisor describes and accounts for events on the placement. It is all the more remarkable because this is her first 'professional' student. Her clarity in the interview is a reflection of the way she approached the placement, pushing both the student and the tutor into being more explicit about their expectations of the placement, especially when faced with the student's lack of specificity:

I guess I started to talk to him about his previous experience, to get some understanding of the level at which he was at that point in time, so I could get a kind of picture of the stage he was, when he was beginning his placement . . . and I married that up with my own expectations of where I thought he should have been . . . [and] where he should be at the end of the placement, and tried to discuss these with [him] and his tutor . . . Basically it seemed like everything was rather hazy, neither [he] nor his tutor had very clear ideas as to what it was that he was wanting to achieve in a final placement.

She decided that this vagueness and lack of clarity might push her into a more directive role, at least at first, so she tried to establish his stage of development:

I had my own expectations, though that wasn't married very closely with [the student's] expectations, nor his tutor's. Their side of it all seemed very hazy to me. I took a much more assertive role . . . It was quite structured, but it was necessary for me to get some gauge of [his] ability, to get some sort of baseline for myself to know where he was . . . I also had a lot of anxieties about his actual level of competence, and therefore felt that I needed to be very involved as a supervisor, and probably if necessary quite directive.

This chosen strategy was not, apparently, the only one which the supervisor had considered, in response to her perceptions of the student's learning needs and her expectations derived from her own student experience:

At the beginning of the placement I was extremely directive, and stated very clearly what my expectations were, and from that basis [we] began to discuss things . . .

Some of the student's initial response was to reject her suggestions. He felt visits to local agencies were a waste of time because he 'knew' what all such agencies were like. There are two aspects of this which are of interest – one was his denial of the value of personal contact with other agencies (a view which he revised by the end of the placement). The other is his view of agencies being the same, no matter where they were located, which fits with his vague generalizations in setting goals for the placement.

The supervisor's early directiveness, and explicit contract goals for the placement were something of a challenge for the student, but he was highly motivated to pass, and had decided on the least risky way of achieving that – by acquiescence, and following what his teacher required of him.

The supervisor is able to see how this pattern, of directive teaching and a passive student, had changed during the placement, and points to the importance of a discussion about power and authority in supervision, after which the student felt able to trust her, and to take risks with her support. By the end of the placement she describes the student as having considerable responsibility for his own learning, and for the choice of focus in supervision:

Basically, at the end of the placement [he] made the decisions about how he was going to work, what he was going to do, and I encouraged him and supported him in what he was doing . . . if he had areas of difficulty, we discussed those in depth . . . [how he could use] different ways of resolving a problem . . . so the relationship became much more balanced.

The turning points in the balance of the supervisory relationship arise from the student being able to trust the supervisor (and take risks in his practice) which were already showing signs of change prior to the point at which there was a death in the office. The supervisor describes the change from directive teaching and passive learning to a more consultative model:

> He, with little guidance from me after planning the initial contact, planning the first visit . . . made a plan which we discussed in supervision, and after that point he basically did his own planning and intervention . . . My role in supervision was mainly to praise what he had done, to encourage him, to broaden out what he had done and put what he had done into a more rounded picture . . . if he came to any areas where he was stuck, we would discuss those.

As a result of this shift in the pattern of the teaching and learning processes, the student is able to be more caring and creative in his work, as the episode involving the move of an elderly man into Part Three accommodation illustrated. This introduction of caring, into what previously had been a more mechanistic approach to practice, followed the period of grief and mourning in the office. There appears to be a close connection between how the student saw the learning task, with the need to be more actively involved in his learning and how he practised.

The student appeared to have undertaken the previous eighteen months of the course with a model in which others (i.e. teachers) would be responsible for his learning, by being in authority, and having expertise. This echoes some of the early positions described by Perry (1970) which were reviewed earlier, in terms of the student not yet having reached a stage of understanding the importance of context, and the relativism of all knowledge, as a precondition for taking responsibility for his own learning.

The supervisor explicitly acknowledged in her interview the parallels between how the student learnt on this placement, and how she had learnt in her own placements as a student:

> We both work best from a structured framework, we both need the theoretical input as well as the practice, and are able to integrate the two . . . a little bit of practice, then a little bit of theory . . .

Finally, the supervisor stresses her role as part of a team of other potential teachers, to whom the student can turn for help, and to whom he has things to offer. This reciprocity is an extension of the two way nature of the supervision relationship itself:

> . . . he used other people in my office, that I wasn't the only person . . . he made use of, and was used by others in our Department [she gave an example relating to the new Mental Health Act] . . . At the beginning it was decided that he would do some work with elderly clients, and I didn't have any [clients, and expertise] . . . I suggested others in the office had a lot of experience and it would be better to discuss with them. That's a common

theme running right through, I'd point something out, he was motivated to try it out . . . the team were helpful, but people felt he'd given as much as he'd gained, it was two way.

In summary, this interview reveals a supervisor whose clarity and explicitness set the scene for a structured and focused use of supervision, and clear intervention by the student with his clients. The supervisor chooses to be controlling in the early stages, and does some direct teaching. The student was initially passive, and expecting his teacher to take responsibility for his learning, but he increasingly took responsibility for his own learning, and the relationship became more equal. These changes result from a shift in the supervisory relationship, which allows the student to take more risks in his work and learning, knowing that he will be supported by his supervisor. On her part, there is a shift from directive teaching, to a more consultative style of supervision, and preparedness to use others in the office to contribute to teaching.

Later, in developing a model from the findings, these interactive patterns are used as key indicators of the *stage* of development reached by supervisors and students in their conceptions of learning.

5.2.3   *Joint discussion with the student and supervisor*

After each pair of interviews in this phase of the research, an opportunity was offered to the participants to discuss the Clobbits learning styles exercise, and to relate the findings from it to the discussions in the interviews. That session was also an opportunity to offer as feedback something of the research findings so far, and to clarify what had been generated in these interviews.

During the interviews in this example, it was decided to ask whether they would object to the feedback session being taped as well. There were two reasons for this request: first was that the feedback sessions undertaken earlier in this phase of the study had raised interesting issues, including the use of the session by the participants to discuss and reframe their understanding of some events in the placement; second was that the clarity and articulate accounts of this placement suggested it would be valuable to tape the feedback session. They agreed to do so.

A further purpose of the feedback session, of clarifying some interpretations, and checking them out with the participants, is also well-demonstrated here.

The researcher opened the session with some comments on the Clobbits exercise generally, and in relation to the approaches they had used. The supervisor had used a holist, and the student a serialist, strategy. There was an exchange between the student and his supervisor about aspects of learning on the placement.

The student said, 'I think the learning style you expected me to possess was problem-solving, starting at the top and working your way down to specific behaviours, which you wrote down more than the higher order behaviours.' The supervisor responded as she seems to have done from the earliest part of the placement: 'What do you mean by that?' and got the reply: 'You wrote down specific things more than general things . . . in setting up the contract'.

The supervisor said 'I wanted specific entities as a basis for the contract, which could be worked on and evaluated at the end, rather than generalities that couldn't be defined or evaluated very easily.' 'Which was appropriate', replied the student.

The researcher offered some input about the importance of being able to generalize from specific examples and being able to use generalizations in new situations, where they may be appropriate. Being able to sort out levels of generality and specificity was very important, if you were going to be able to make use of past learning in new situations. It seemed that an intervening stage, of being able to generalize from earlier experiences, was most helpful in making sense of the new situation.

The student responded by indicating that at the beginning of the placement he had felt that client contracts were boring because they were all the same. The supervisor responded: 'That's because you needed to make them individual, and specific to that client . . . [it was also] tied into assessment and planning at a more general level, so the contract related to the assessment and where you wanted to go', indicating that progress had been made in that area.

The discussion in the interview with the student was raised, notably about how the supervisor 'had made a learning assessment of you and where you were, perhaps using her previous experience as a learner and a student . . . maybe we can ask her how she did it . . . and what were the indications you used as evidence?' The supervisor said that it was to do with 'how clear he was [or wasn't] about his expectations of the final placement . . . [laughing, in a self-mocking kind of way] because I'd known what I wanted for my final placement, and thought everyone else should as well!' The researcher added: 'and explicitly, and in specific terms!' and got the reply 'Absolutely!' with laughter.

She continued: 'It was also his understanding of theory and practice of the social work process – I thought he'd know more . . .' The student asked 'How, in the placement, when I'd done some visits, and we'd have supervision, I said earlier, that you'd always seemed to be one step ahead of me', only to be told by the supervisor 'That's just 'cos I'm smarter than you!' with more laughter. The student said: 'On what basis did you assess my learning need . . . did you say perhaps we are going to broaden this, or . . . how did you work it out. I'm suggesting you did it like the process you went through.'

The supervisor said, 'Yes, I guess modelling, that was part of it, on what my own supervisors did for me . . . [but] some was just sequential, in your work with a client [she describes phases in the work, of initial contact, making an assessment, making a plan and sharing it with the client, and so on] . . . whatever we'd talked about in supervision, by the next time you'd done it, you'd done it well and appropriately . . . so that was step by step.'

The student said 'I've gone from A to B on this placement . . . [If that were] numbered one to ten, when we'd got to seven, how did you know eight was next . . . ?'

The supervisor said, 'Most of it was intuitive, I think . . . but we had goals set for the end . . . in the contract . . . so that was the direction . . . In terms of whether I generalized, it was in terms of whether I *could* generalize, if I knew my theory well enough. There were certain points at which you couldn't handle the generalization because you weren't far enough on in terms of your practice, and your conceptualizations, so it had to be left. But as you did more work, and perhaps read about things, something else would come together so I could introduce it at that time, make more generalizations at the time . . . [she restates this in different terms] . . . Sometimes you [the student] could handle that, and were aware of that . . . it was your ability to conceptualize that led to progress. I just tried to round it out.' The student restated this in his own words, then said: 'That's why you were one step ahead of me! Because I had done these bits [the specifics] and you could help me generalize.'

There was further discussion around these points, and in response to the researcher, the student stressed the importance of recognizing salience in making patterns and generalizations from experience.

In a closing summary, the researcher thanked the participants for contributing in three areas – research data; some development of the researcher's conceptualizations about supervision; and in allowing him to see that a good outcome could arise from what had been potentially a very difficult placement.

A final discussion, about the involvement of the tutor, and the use of the three-way sessions, led to the suggestion that she should be interviewed as well, to get a further perspective on the placement.

Because the data gathered in the primary interviews were so clear and explicit, it was decided that using the material as a case study could be enhanced by interviewing the tutor. The tutor readily agreed, and that material is reported next. This was the only placement in which the role and involvement of the tutor was raised directly as a contribution to teaching and learning.

It is evident that many of the researcher's views on the teaching and learning being described were expressed during the joint interview, therefore there are no additional comments offered at this point. Instead, the more general issues which were raised by this placement are discussed in the interview with the tutor, in the next section.

5.2.4   *Interview with the tutor; and general comments on case illustration I*

This interview took place shortly after the end of the placement, at the College where the student had completed his course. The tutor, who was very experienced in social work education, was interested to contribute to the research. The interview itself lasted about one and a half hours, and was a mixture of discussion about the individual placement, issues raised by it, and by the research more generally. The format follows that pattern, with a report of the interview (included as indented paragraphs) interspersed by wider considerations prompted by the interview.

> The interview began with an invitation to describe the placement chronologically, from the tutor's point of view. She recounted considerable difficulty in setting up a placement for this student, with two prior arrangements falling through in other agencies. The student had been asking for a further placement in a social services department, after some criticisms of his work last year. The tutor described the student as 'bright, very bright [i.e. intelligent], but incredibly backward, unaccountably backward . . . and needing [as a supervisor] someone who could cope with him intellectually.' The tutor described the first three-way meeting at the college, '. . . when [the supervisor] came with a great many questions', including [according to the tutor] questions about why the student was 'so backward' [tutor's use of language], 'why does he want another social services placement? . . . and by implication, are you landing me with a failing student?'

None of this problem about finding a placement had emerged in the earlier interview, nor any suggestion that the student was under-performing, and had not done well on his previous placement. The supervisor and student had both pointed to a lack of specificity, and uncertainty on the student's and tutor's part about the purpose of the placement.

> The tutor continued by saying, '[The supervisor] was trying to tease out what [he] wanted to learn, and was trying to set objectives for the placement . . . [his] communication skills were horrible . . . [She] was writing a lot down . . . I was really rather impressed, thinking here's someone who might get to grips with [him], and I said so to her . . . [He]'s a puzzle to me . . . so many things didn't add up . . . the first successful ingredient in the placement was that [she] was totally puzzled and asked questions . . .'
>
> The researcher asked the nature of the student's problems at that stage, and was told 'he was very inarticulate in tutorials . . . I was making no progress in helping this student to clarify what he had to learn . . . we [the course staff] tended to blame the seconding department . . . [because of problems with a previous student from that agency] . . . he was a Level Two social worker, and he's bright, but he's incompetent. I was questioning his motivation for social work, wondering why he was in social work at all . . . did he have the capacity . . . he had his own frame of reference, and he rejected psycho-dynamic approaches . . . his first year placement, he had a very poor assessment, he had a social control model, there were some

cases he closed very early . . . I think [this supervisor] underestimated how bad [he] was.'

The researcher asked how he had passed the year one assessment if he was so limited, and was told 'It's a good question . . . it was very short, only eleven weeks . . . no, he wasn't failing, but he wasn't quite achieving . . . I thought his first supervisor had done quite well in challenging, stopping him in his tracks . . . he wasn't that marginal, it was a poorly written report . . . I think a lot of our students in the first year are marginal . . . we've never had someone who failed a first year placement . . . he's bright [and people say] he's a nice guy.'

The researcher said, 'I think it's often described as a learning, or developmental problem, in the first year rather than failing . . . it tends to be put off to the second year.' The tutor said 'I don't think you *can* fail a first year placement.'

This exchange points to the more general problem of practice assessment: there is little clarity about what should be expected of students at the end of a first year placement. There are some remarkable terms (derived from the classical model) the tutor uses to describe the student, like 'incredibly backward, unaccountably backward' and 'he was very inarticulate in tutorials'. The tutor thought, 'no, he wasn't failing, but he wasn't quite achieving', and 'he wasn't that marginal, it was a poorly written report.' (This, of course, is an assessment of the supervisor, not the student). The interview continued:

[He] was a person not able to talk about himself . . . he didn't know what he wanted to learn. I was put on my mettle. [The supervisor] was making demands on me, in a positive way. She was *quite anxious*, it was her first student . . . [as a result of her pressure] I had to deliver the goods but I didn't know what they'd be . . . [She] wrote out the contract.

At the three-way meeting in the middle of the placement, there had been a discussion about the student's lack of competence [rather than what his first year supervisor had described as a lack of confidence]. After some pressing by the researcher, about the tutor's view of an adequate workload for a student, the tutor said:

[The supervisor] *taught* him the social work process, which we had failed to do . . . she has an exceptionally good grasp, she must have been *well-taught*, I guess [her course] was better than ours . . . She comes across in a way that she really knows what she's doing, in a way that a lot of our supervisors don't. She'd got it well together and *taught* it to him. The researcher asked 'How?' The tutor said 'By quite a lot of direct *teaching*, and analysis before [the student] went out in terms of where he was in the process.' (emphases added)

The added emphases here make the point about use of language identified in the review of the traditional literature on supervision, where the focus was on *teaching and what was taught*, rather than on *learning and what was learnt*. The tutor described a change in the way the college had *taught* social work to this group of students, and acknowledged that perhaps students had not grasped essentials. Her model is to describe this student's learning in terms of the supervisor's *teaching* (positively), and college *teaching* (negatively). However, it would seem from the evidence of the individual interviews, and the joint interview, that it was the supervisor's attention to the student's *learning* processes, and particularly to the timing of her contributions (in relation to her assessment of his stage of learning) that was a major factor in the outcome of the placement.

It is also worth considering how the tutor viewed this first time supervisor – there are some indications that she was surprised about the supervisor's competence in the role, and she ascribes this to the supervisor having been *well-taught* herself. The social work education literature after this placement took place gives some support for the view that it is a *learning* focus, rather than a *teaching* focus which is critical in helping students to learn effectively, and to learn how they learn, so they can take responsibility for their own learning (e.g. Gardiner 1984b; Gray 1985). These ideas are discussed further and developed in Chapter 7.

This interpretation is further borne out by the tutor's description of the student as a passive learner, trying to meet the expectations of others:

> He said, at the end, that he was playing games, trying to fulfil the expectations of others . . . in tutorials he was trying to meet my expectations . . . his approach was revolutionized in the placement, by [the supervisor] appearing human, real and in need . . . [he] could get out of being the student, they were both out of role . . . [because] she was a highly professional person and teacher [it led to him getting] his personal and professional side of himself together . . . he said that the crisis forced him to adopt new coping strategies . . . [and] less direct teaching forced him to work things out for himself.

There followed an exchange which was more discursive, and involved the researcher reflecting on his experience as a supervisor, and some of the findings of the present research, which was offered to the tutor to allow her to reframe some of her descriptions, [in relation to stages of development of students, and the importance of the learning process]. The tutor acknowledged the validity of these comments, and began to relate them to the placement under discussion. They are not detailed here to maintain the confidentiality of the course and tutor.

In essence, some of the debate was about the ways in which students view the learning tasks, and the consequent role they expect to play in that learning. In this instance, the student entered the final placement still with an expectation that he should be the passive recipient of teaching, and that his task was to fit in with the expectations of his teachers. This had apparently been reinforced during his previous placements, in college teaching, and in tutorials.

This is perhaps not unconnected with his instrumental and mechanistic view of social work, without personal involvement, which had persisted until the middle of this placement. As he became aware of the need to be more involved in one domain (learning), so he was able to develop similarly in the other (practice). The placement saw the development of the student's conception of the learning process from one where he saw learning as something external, which happened to him, towards learning as something which involved him, and became part of him. This change reflects the steps in the development of the learning process described earlier (Saljo 1979), and is one which shifts the focus of attention in learning from *content* to *process*.

In parallel, the supervisor allowed and encouraged this development, even before the death in the office crystallized and confirmed the process. At this stage in the research, it was becoming clear that if the supervisor had not herself already reached the stage of being able to conceptualise the learning processes in terms at least as far as the student was now reaching, it may seriously have hampered his progress. A very good example of the constraining impact of a supervisor's conception of learning is given in the next case illustration.

There is evidently a need to pay attention to the stage which the supervisor has reached as a teacher (which is related to the stage they have reached in their conceptions and understanding of learning). The supervisor in this case study had a mature conception of the learning required of professional social work students, and thus was able to make an informed judgement about where the student had reached in his stage of learning, as well as his practice competence. Although she was very explicit about many aspects of the placement, this was one area where she described her response as 'intuitive' and based on an internalized understanding of conceptions of learning. She was not then able to conceptualise these features after a single experience of supervising a professional placement. It was decided to follow her up after she had next supervised a student to see whether it was possible to find further evidence of these stages of development as a teacher. She did indeed show that she could be much less directive, and less prescriptive, with a more able student.

Returning to the interview with the tutor, the discussion moved on to the point where the researcher offered a routine opportunity to say whether there were other things which the tutor wished to talk about that had not previously been covered. She said that she wanted to talk about the unjustified criticism of the first year supervisor, contained in this supervisor's placement report:

> 'I want to say something about [the supervisor's] criticism of the year one supervisor . . .' The researcher said 'Perhaps it was something to do with different styles of the two supervisors?' 'Yes, [the other one] was much less intellectual than [this supervisor], *less able to teach* than [her] . . . if she had been the second year supervisor as well, they wouldn't have got much further . . .' (emphasis added).

This exchange reflects the tutor apparently contradicting herself, by at first thinking the criticism was unjust, but then giving the reasons why it could be fair criticism. During that exchange, I gained the distinct impression that the tutor felt that she too was implicitly being criticized for failing to confront the student, and then help him to move on. This view is reinforced by a later exchange in the interview:

'He was very difficult . . . thank goodness I was his tutor for two years [normal practice was to change at the end of the first year] . . . It wasn't really until [the supervisor] came along . . . [it was] her really strong questioning of obvious things that didn't add up . . .' The researcher said '[The supervisor] had avoided over-teaching in the second half of the placement as [the student] took more responsibility for his learning, unlike some supervisors . . .' The tutor was reluctant to acknowledge this, feeling that as a new supervisor, '[she] was only forced out of a pattern of direct teaching by the death in the office, and by being forced out of pattern to be seen as a human being'. The researcher said that there was evidence in the other interviews to indicate that the shift in teaching and learning, in the supervisory relationship, had already begun before the death, which had only crystallized out what was starting to happen anyway. The tutor said she thought '[the supervisor] was only not over-teaching intuitively.'

This exchange shows the extent to which the researcher is not a passive, and detached observer, but is directly offering evidence to the tutor about the placement (gleaned from the earlier interviews) to challenge the tutor's conception of events. It is worth emphasizing that student and supervisor had explicitly given permission for anything which had been covered in the interviews to be discussed both in the joint session, and in the interview with the tutor.

It is arguable here that the researcher got drawn into challenging the tutor's belief that her perception in such situations was inevitably more 'real' than those directly involved. This view, as we have seen, is characteristic of the classical model, where tutors have traditionally set themselves up to be arbiters of reality and fantasy in the supervisory relationship, even when they were not themselves actually present (Garrett 1954).

Before moving on to other case illustrations, which are presented in less detail, the findings of the present case study are summarized in terms which take forward thinking about the teaching and learning processes of supervision, and which begin the process of model building grounded in the data of this study.

5.3 Key themes and interpretations – first steps towards model building

There are a number of themes derived from this case example which are of major importance to the study. They contribute substantially to the theory-building process, and are considered here in some detail to identify (and generalize from) features of this placement which recur elsewhere. The data include evidence of the persistence of the classical model of supervision, of the movement and change in the patterns of the supervisory relationship, and of the impact of assessment on learning.

5.3.1   *The persistence of the classical model*

The persistence of the language and concepts of the classical supervision model is demonstrated in the interview with the tutor, which shows a number of the central features of the model which was outlined earlier. These include the focus on teaching (rather than learning), the pathologizing of the learner, and the limited expectations tutors have of new supervisors. This very experienced tutor seems to have internalized many of the assumptions and expectations contained in the classical literature:

The focus on teaching
. . . the tutor said, '[the supervisor] *taught* him the social work process, which we had failed to do . . . she has an exceptionally good grasp, she must have been *well-taught*, I guess [her course] was better than ours . . . She comes across in a way that she really knows what she's doing in a way that a lot of supervisors don't. She'd got it well together and *taught* it to him.' The researcher asked 'How?' The tutor said, 'By quite a lot of direct *teaching* . . .' (emphases added).

The pathologizing of the learner
The tutor described the student as 'bright, very bright [i.e. intelligent], but incredibly backward, unaccountably backward . . . and needing [as a supervisor] someone who could cope with him intellectually . . . [his] communication skills were horrible . . . [She] was writing a lot down . . . I was really rather impressed, thinking here's someone who might get to grips with [him], and I said so to her . . . [He's] a puzzle to me . . . so many things didn't add up.'

The expectations of new supervisors
'I think [the supervisor] underestimated how bad [he] was . . . [the supervisor] was forced out of a pattern of direct teaching by a death in the office . . . she was only not over-teaching intuitively . . .'

5.3.2   *Movement and change in the supervisory relationship – the student's conceptions of learning*

Changes in the pattern of interaction between student and the supervisor in various phases of the placement are evident. (The term *phase* is used here to describe periods during the placement. The term *stage* is used to refer to the development of the student's and supervisor's conceptions of learning). At the beginning of the placement, the student's conception of learning is that he expected others to take responsibility for his learning. He was a *passive learner* and seeing *learning as something which would happen to him*. He saw his *supervisor as having expertise* (as a social worker), and *authority* (derived from expertise, and her power to pass or fail him). This position reflects the early positions in Perry's scheme of development (Perry 1970), and of surface conceptions of learning (Saljo 1979). The student decided at that point *he would do what the supervisor required of him in order that he should pass*. He expected to *learn first and do things (i.e. apply learning) afterwards*. This position seems also to be associated with an *instrumental or mechanistic model of social work practice* which avoids involvement in and with his cases.

These emphasized components of this conception of learning will be called *Stage One* here. This position is associated with a belief in a single, right way to learn (and, in the practice domain, with the belief that there is a single, right way to practise) – both of which minimize personal risk and involvement in the process.

The student moved during the placement to seeing more *active involvement in his own learning* as important, and he now sees himself as better in this respect. He says that *he would not be passive in future, and would not give such responsibility to others*. This is evidenced by his preparations for returning to his employing authority. Some of the movement and change has come about as a result of explicit discussions in supervision about power and authority, and a decision by the student to trust his supervisor that she would not unreasonably fail him. She agreed to give him continuous feedback on his performance during the placement. *The recognition that he had power* (to pass and fail) as a result of his performance seems to have contributed to his increased involvement in his learning and in his practice. The realization that there might be *other ways to approach learning*, followed by the *attempt to use another approach* seem to be important features of *Stage Two*.

This stage also seems to have parallel changes in the practice domain – the student made important changes following his changed conceptions of learning. First, he felt able to bring more warmth and caring into his practice, which meant that he was less detached from his clients, freeing him to do more sensitive work with them. Second, he began to develop additional frames of reference in assessment and intervention with his clients.

In this second stage, the student was still reliant to some extent on his tutor and supervisor to reinforce and validate the changed approaches, so they can be described as *increased involvement in his learning, and in his practice, but not complete autonomy*. A further feature seems to have been increased confidence for the student, and real enjoyment in his work and learning.

5.3.3 Movement and change in the supervisory relationship – the supervisor's conceptions of learning

The supervisor's conceptions of learning were initially different from those of the student. She began by looking for clarity and explicitness which she modelled in drawing up the contract. She appeared to expect that the student's *learning would arise from doing* things, whereas he expected to be learning things first, and doing things afterwards.

These differences in their conceptions of the learning process also demonstrate the difference between active and passive learning. They were confirmed by the findings of the Clobbits exercise, where the student had difficulty in holding a large number of variables/hypotheses in his head, which Pask suggests relates to the lower risk-taking of serialist strategies. The supervisor used a holist approach, and was able to tolerate a higher degree of uncertainty in her learning. Learning from one's own practice experience in social work is in these terms, a holist, and active kind of learning, which the supervisor sees as necessary if one is to build up generalizations from patterns in one's practice.

The supervisor made an assessment of the student's competence early on and, like the supervisor in the single case study, became more *directive in her teaching*, until she was sure that the student was able to function competently with clients. This pattern *allowed the student to be dependent* on the direction of his supervisor initially, but her demands for explicitness, and for specificity, seem to have produced a crisis and led to the debate about power in the relationship. Later in the placement, the supervisor increasingly *encouraged the student to take responsibility for determining the use of supervision*, and for *making decisions in his cases*.

To characterize the elements of the placement from the supervisor's perspective, *Stage One*, shows a more traditional, directive teacher taking responsibility to assure herself of the student's current level of functioning before encouraging him to be more actively involved in his own learning. In *Stage Two*, she demonstrated that there are other ways to teach, and other ways to learn. She became less directive once she was reasonably sure of the student's competence.

In the second half of the placement, the supervisor demonstrated that teachers need to develop a repertoire of approaches, to respond to differing needs of the student at different points. Sometimes she provided direct teaching when it was required (in relation to the sculpting incident) and sometimes helped the student to recognize patterns and to generalize his experiences (in the discussion in the feedback interview). The role of the supervisor as teacher in this placement, and the interactive patterns, confirm a more general point made by Entwistle (1987):

> Lecturers thus play a crucial role, not just in transmitting information efficiently, but also in transforming ways of learning which would otherwise prevent personal understanding being attempted, let alone achieved. What students perceive as good 'teaching' will, of course, depend on their own conceptions of learning . . .

This will be true for the development of teachers, as well as for students. Another feature of the supervisor's teaching approach was the recognition that she was not an expert in everything, and therefore she was willing to encourage the student to learn from other members of the office team – especially in relation to those areas of her work where she was less experienced. Such an approach could be seen as a relatively early position in thinking about teaching and learning (using Other Experts as Authorities), but in this case it is associated with the encouragement of reciprocity, and the student contributing to the team about new legislation he had studied in college.

This valuing and giving status to the student is a further example of her empowering him, following the supervision discussion about trust and power. Her confidence in her role, and her lack of feeling threatened by the student, is exemplified in the feedback discussion by her use of humour in response to his questions about how she knew what the next steps in his learning should be: 'That's just 'cos I'm smarter than you!' The supervisor in the earlier single case study seemed at times to be more threatened by that student, and retained rather tighter control in supervision.

It would not be proper to leave this discussion about movement and change in the placement without reference to the effect of the death of the social worker who had been a member of the team until her illness. Clearly it had a significant impact on the team, and on the placement. However, careful questioning in the interviews would suggest that although its impact was to crystallize out many of the changes rather more quickly than might otherwise have been the case, it is evident that it was not that crisis alone which precipitated the changes. The key discussions about authority in supervision, and the changes (in how the supervisor and student operated) were underway at the time of the death.

The choice of teaching approach shown by the supervisor, and her response to the student's learning needs could be argued as substituting one right way for another (as the tutor appeared to believe). Therefore, later in the study, it was decided to follow up this supervisor to consider whether she could demonstrate a repertoire of teaching approaches in other circumstances. This was done, more than two years later, when she had next supervised a student. The diversity of approach was maintained, with evidence of a less directive, more democratic relationship from an early point in the placement. It is perhaps indicative of the difficulty of developing supervisory skills (despite the shortage of·supervisors) that this promising new supervisor did not have another student for more than two years after the end of the placement reported here.

5.3.4 *The impact of assessment on learning*

The review of research into adult learning showed that assessment and other contextual factors can have a significant influence on the nature and quality of student learning (Laurillard 1978; Saljo 1979). The placement just described, and the earlier single case study, show the constraining effect of a supervisor's doubts about student competence on teaching and learning processes because they encourage more directive teaching.

The next chapter reports some other case examples and looks at the extent to which the preliminary statement of *stages of conceptions of learning* outlined above can contribute to understanding. The first of these is a particularly striking example of the influence of assessment on learning processes, where an experienced supervisor, with a traditional approach to teaching, is supervising a student who fails.

6

The Anatomy of Supervision:
Some Further Case Examples

6.1 Case illustration II – a failed placement

This case illustration is an example of problems in the supervisory relationship which contribute to a premature end of the placement. The student failed, and left social work altogether. Therefore, uniquely in this study, there is no matching interview of the student – but the supervisor's interview graphically demonstrates problems in supervision, so is included here. This experienced full-time supervisor came to social work as a mature student, in a second career. He works in a statutory agency.

The supervisor chose this placement, which had recently ended, to be interviewed about (even though there were other current placements he could have discussed), because he thought it had been an important learning experience for him. He had completed the questionnaire and was followed up as a result. The student was undertaking an additional placement, having previously failed his final placement on a University post-graduate course.

6.1.1 The student's 'pathology' and the classical model

The interview begins with the supervisor describing 'difficulties' at the start of the placement. He twice describes the student as 'a lad', even though he was thirty-six years old. It perhaps indicates how the supervisor saw him. The supervisor began by describing his early impressions:

> . . . things that I think were particular difficulties for him were the fact that he felt the kind of developmental, Freudian approach was meaningless, he couldn't see that he needed that, that it was relevant to the work he was being asked to do . . .

The supervisor offers this as an indication of difficulties for the student, but is in fact describing a difference of view about one, somewhat traditional approach to social casework. In the rest of the interview there were no examples of continuing work where such an approach could have been developed. Instead, much of the work seemed to be writing court reports.

It is possible, of course, to explain the exchange in a different way. The model used by the supervisor locates cause, and responsibility, for the 'difficulty' with (or within) the student. The supervisor clearly takes for granted the relevance of such an approach, and does not offer the student room to express an alternative. There is one right way to approach social work for this supervisor – the 'Freudian approach'.

In the previous case example, the supervisor encouraged the student to take risks in trying out new approaches to his work, offered some alternative strategies when the student had made a client assessment, and specific teaching to back up the student's choice. There seems to be an important distinction here between the expectation that there is a single, right way to practise, and the recognition of diversity of responses to client need.

6.1.2   The assessment of practice competence

The supervisor goes on to describe a further 'difficulty' in similar ways:

> The other one was . . . the criterion 'practice must submit to the discipline of results' and this got him very worried, because he said 'what if my clients don't show any results?' . . .

The 'difficulty' here is of the same kind: the supervisor is asserting a position which he believes to be the right one. The student does not appear to agree, and this is seen as a difficulty for the student. There were examples of this kind of problem in the descriptions of the researcher's own student experience earlier.

Whittington and Holland (1985) point to the difficulties which can arise from students and supervisors having different implicit models and assumptions about the activity of social work itself. They see the making explicit of assumptions as 'an objective of each student embarking on qualifying training' and they continue, later:

> In making sense of situations we impose ideas or constructs on those situations . . . [and] it has long been plain that there is no theoretical consensus in social work. The absence of theoretical concensus disqualifies theoretical 'training' or apprenticeship; instead the plurality of theories in contemporary social work and the conflicts between them necessitate 'education' for students, and again, exploratory roles for the participants [i.e. tutors, supervisors and students].

It may be, in future, that major contributions in this area will come from black students and social workers. At the time of writing there is concern about how white teachers assess black students. Many formulations pathologize the student (especially where the development of black perspectives on social work represent a fundamental challenge to prevailing orthodoxy) rather than recognizing the interactive nature of such situations, and the lack of theoretical consensus.

The supervisor felt that if clients don't change, then the social work input is 'a waste of time', and that this would be an indication the student was failing. However, social work intervention in this placement seems to have consisted largely of assessing family situations and providing reports for courts. In such situations, client change might not be the best indication of the quality or effectiveness of the social work undertaken.

> As the interview continues, the supervisor goes on to describe his expectation about when it is possible to evaluate a placement. 'In the working agreement, it had been made quite clear, and I do see this as a general practice, that it would not be possible to say until fairly close to the end of it whether the student was passing it or failing the placement.'

Later in the interview, his description of the process which is actually gone through contradicts this assertion. Clarity about the nature and method of assessment is essential, not only in terms of fairness and justice for the students, but also in relation to the impact which the assessment of learning has on the student's learning (Saljo 1975). One can only conjecture what the student felt in the circumstance where he has already failed his final placement, and now (on appeal) is allowed one further opportunity to pass the course. The timing of the assessment seems unclear, and the supervisor has a value position in relation to methods of working, and the outcomes of work, which conflict with those of the student. The researcher asked what the student was meant to be learning on the placement:

> In the working agreement, we had spelt out the areas in which he was going to be assessed, and I really do that from the stages of the social work process, so I've really got eight stages . . . number one is that you have to show you can conduct interviews, gather information, and make relationships . . . number two, and here I would quarrel a little bit with the CCETSW Guidelines, because they don't seem to me to be in any logical order . . . (He continued with eight such areas.)

The reference to the CCETSW Guidelines is interesting, because they describe a number of areas in which students must demonstrate competence (CCETSW 1981). They are not intended to be construed as in sequential order, because they describe things of very different levels of generality and specificity, and of overlapping focus. For example, some relate to knowledge of the law, and social welfare provisions, whilst others describe core social work practice skills.

The search for order by this supervisor is by no means unusual – indeed we all try to order and frame our experiences. However, his comment about the CCETSW Guidelines is interesting when considered alongside his approach to the Clobbits learning styles exercise in which he (uniquely of those completing it during the present study) attempted the exercise in a completely sequential way. This exercise, it should be recalled, involves selecting cards from sets of materials which provide information about a fictitious taxonomy, which has to be learnt. This supervisor began by looking at card A_1, then A_2, A_3, etc, then at B_1, B_2, B_3, etc, through to the final card E_5, because he thought that the numbering and lettering of the cards in sequence showed that to be the right and proper way to do the task.

In turning to the student's performance, the supervisor described how the student was progressing in relation to 'the eight stages of the social work process':

> It seemed from the kind of feedback I was getting, that number one was OK, he was showing that he had certain skills . . . I tend to see knowledge as informing all of those eight stages, and that is how I try to link in his knowledge from his University course . . . [which includes] . . . the principles of casework that Butrym picks up from Biestek . . . he had some skill in it and was at least proceding satisfactorily for that stage of the placement . . .

Here, the supervisor seems to assume that all cases will last to the end of the placement, and that the student's work will progress sequentially through the stages described. Clients' circumstances change so that termination, and evaluation of work undertaken, might be necessary after only a small number of contacts. However, the student does not seem to be required to be able to evaluate his work until towards the end of the placement, because evaluation is apparently towards the end of the eight stages in the model to which the supervisor adheres.

6.1.3   *The learning and teaching processes*

The supervisor said that the student produced a good deal of undifferentiated material in his reports:

> We ran into difficulties straight away because he had a lot of difficulties separating what was relevant from what was not relevant, you'd just get a mass of material . . .

This supervisor sees as 'difficulties' exactly what the supervisor in the previous case illustration saw as material indicating that the student needed help to recognize commonalities, and patterns in his work, so he could begin to generalize; and she described the importance of timing such teaching. This full-time supervisor, with a focus on what was to be taught, apparently did not see it as part of his role to help the student in the process of learning. The supervisor described the student as 'demanding':

> I'm different here with this student, usually just an hour a week, but with this lad, I spent an hour and a half a week and other occasions as well – so he demanded a lot of time, he couldn't understand why he was a demanding student . . .

Again, comparison with the previous case example is instructive: there was usually supervision for one and a half to two hours, and the supervisor felt that she was not pulling her full weight after the death of her colleague when she could only see the student during supervision sessions.

The next part of this interview illuminates the supervisor's teaching approach:

> So we had difficulties with the writing, I had to *rewrite* two social enquiry reports, and I was quite prepared to do that because I thought that *it is from this that he quite hopefully is learning*, and I was interested to see what he did learn . . . He produced a quite impressive list – of ten points – of what he did learn. He had other reports to do, and *those began to need less correction . . .* (emphases added).

The supervisor has a model, apparently, of the teacher as an expert, and of the student as an apprentice. There is also a little of the school-teacher here in the use of terms like 'rewrite', and 'need less correction'. The student was criticized for cue-seeking, using other social enquiry reports as a model, to get things 'right' in the eyes of the supervisor:

> . . . He was trying to copy from previous reports, trying to get it right, but he hadn't got the imagination . . .

The supervisor then stresses that he thinks not only that there is something wrong, but that *there is something wrong with the student* which is '*a measure of his disturbance*'. It seems as if he sees the student as a client, with 'his difficulties', and 'his disturbance', and, later he and the tutor had wondered 'is he mad?':

> So the writing work was improving. Aha, this was relevant here. He couldn't write in a legible way, at least I couldn't read it, it really was very poor. So he used to type, but because that was disturbing to the social worker with whom he used to share, so he used to type at home at nights . . . That was a real difficulty, but as he settled down, his writing improved, became quite legible, but that wasn't until after the first three months . . . [and as an aside, almost confidentially] I think that was a measure of his disturbance.

This pathologizing of the student again reproduces the model in the classical literature, where problems in supervision raise doubts about the student's 'educability' (Towle 1954).

The special problems of students who are required to repeat part of their course become graphically clear:

> Then when I came back, the student said he was terribly tired, and I mean it really was an unhappy situation, because he hadn't got a course he could relate to, he was living in [the University] Hall, pretty much on his own, he didn't have friends here, he said I've got to go back to [his home town].

But, despite these pressures, the student is expected to cope with some additional work, with short deadlines, and explicit threat of failure. Not only does the supervisor act as a traditional teacher, but uses his authority in a controlling way:

[To see how he worked under pressure] I asked him to take on two more reports; he refused. I said if you don't, you'll fail the placement. He said that was an inappropriate comment after all the work he'd done. I did admit that . . . We got [the tutor] in to try to sort it all out, but I think from that stage, anger began to build up . . . [He] did two more reports. Of these, the first was not too bad, the next one was quite unacceptable, and I checked it out with three other seniors . . . so that I wasn't being arbitrary, so we had a consensus. So I rewrote it.

. . . they felt everything he did was in a learning stage, that there was no evidence of his applying learning and knowledge that he had. They felt his contributions in the team had been inappropriate . . . [for example] he wrote up his views on a case that two other social workers had been discussing in the office. It made them very, very angry.

Again, it is possible to interpret these events in other ways than as evidence of the student's pathology. The relationship between theory and practice in social work is not like traditional scientific theory, and it is difficult (in relation to writing court reports) to imagine how Freudian theory will be 'applied'. The student's attempt to construe meaning from other kinds of cases, and learn for himself from them, is offered as evidence of 'everything he did was in a learning stage' which the supervisor seemingly finds unacceptable! The interviewer decided to change tack, and focus on the possibility of supervising in other ways:

(*Interviewer*) If you had another student like that, again, what do you think you would do differently?

Link into the team more . . . as a general practice, I'd want to be more in touch with the team, not so they were spying on him, just helping me with the assessment . . . I need to be more involved in the team, they only learn about me at team meetings, or through the student.

The interviewer asked about alternatives more explicitly:

(*Interviewer*) Do you think that if they [the team] have been involved, at least to some extent, in the assessment bit of the process, there might also be a way that you could involve them in the teaching process . . . they'd be part of the teaching range of resources there, not just part of the assessment . . . they'd be seen as positive by the student, and you and your activity might be more integrated in the team . . .

Yes, yes in theory that is right. Yes. We have had that one a bit . . . could I as a supervisor make any direct input into the teams. It's tied up with credibility, and I'm not sure that I would have anything to offer . . . there wasn't really much I could offer in a teaching capacity.

(*Interviewer*) Yes, mmm. I was wondering what *they* could offer as a *teacher* to the student, as *co-teachers* with you, to the student.

Yes, yes, right [dubiously].

The involvement, or lack of it, by the rest of the social work team here is in marked contrast to the position in Case Illustration I, where they were constructively involved in giving to (and receiving from) the student. Despite the prompting from the interviewer, it took a little time for the supervisor to grasp what this might mean, since it appeared not to have occurred to him before. This is perhaps related to the very individualized model he has of supervision, and to his role as the teacher. It is perhaps all the more surprising when one considers that this experienced, specialist supervisor routinely supervises students (as in this case), in offices other than his own, where the direct involvement of other workers might have been expected to be the norm.

This supervisor, with his belief in a single, right way to practise, and to supervise, is very different from the supervisor described in the last chapter who began from a recognition that there is a variety of ways to supervise. A repertoire of teaching approaches (or at least recognizing there are various ways of teaching) clearly does not come about simply as the result of more supervision experience, nor of having more students. Diversity is therefore more associated with the supervisors' conceptions of learning than the amount of their teaching experience.

In summary, this case illustration is of a supervisor who values individual teaching, who thinks that there is a single body of knowledge to be learned, concerning the right way to practise. This belief in single, right ways to do things, step-by-step, is confirmed by his approach to the Clobbits exercise, and his view of the CCETSW Guidelines.

By contrast, the previous case example showed a supervisor who not only recognized diversity, but encouraged it in the student's practice; and who demonstrated versatility in her own approaches to supervision. Inevitably, a number of comparisons are made between the supervisors, but it is important to note that what is being compared are the approaches they use in a particular supervisory relationship. The Göteburg findings that deep outcomes to learning were not achieved because they were not sought, and not intended, is especially apposite for the supervisor with this failing student, because there he had no conception that the student should actively construe meaning for himself. These ideas are now explored further with some other, briefer case illustrations.

6.2 Case illustration III – an experienced supervisor, and an experienced student

In this example, the supervisor is also a specialist unit supervisor with substantial experience. She had completed the questionnaire exercise. She works in a statutory agency, and had been there for some years, following her social work qualification. The student was an experienced unqualified social worker who had previously trained as a mobility instructor for visually handicapped people.

The interviews took place almost at the end of the final placement in a two year non-graduate course in a University. Less detail of the interaction in the

interview is reported here, and some commentary is interspersed. The interview
with the supervisor was first.

The placement had begun with a selection of work 'intended to sharpen
skills' already possessed by the student, since 'she was seen as a very able
student . . . I felt I needed to test her out in a number of areas. She had very
limited experience of childcare and family work . . .' The early work
'confirmed the impression that she was a very able student'.

The assessment report on the student at the end of her last placement
had suggested that whilst she tends to make good, early assessments in her
cases, this student was somewhat intrusive in goal-setting with her clients
. . . the student 'tended to steer, and sometimes direct, her clients in setting
goals for her intervention . . . She has made a lot of progress in that . . . she
is a very clear and logical thinker . . . she can see things so clearly that there
is a tendency to go in and work with that.'

Again, we see a placement where the supervisor is initially unsure of the
competence of the student, and had decided to establish this early on. The
student acted as a court agent, a traditional caseworker, and a broker of services
in the first weeks of the placement. This demonstration of versatility in her
practice was reassuring to her supervisor, who felt that she was 'very able'. The
question of passing or failing was not apparently going to be much of an issue.
We can see in what follows the impact that this has on the supervisory
relationship, and on the teaching and learning processes.

The student had 'worked sensitively with the family of a terminally ill
cancer patient . . . despite being not very sure about how to use the
assessment she had made . . .'

The interviewer asked 'What did you do in supervision about this?' The
supervisor said, 'I suppose I did the same in supervision . . . as she did in
the case . . . I gave her the chance to talk about her frustrations . . . and
then tried to tie her down later'.

The isomorphism between supervision and practice, which was identified in the
supervision literature, is demonstrated again: the supervisor focuses on the
student's feelings, and acts with her as the student had with the clients. The gap
between the student's assessment of clients and being able to use it was a
continuing issue throughout the placement.

The supervisor went on to describe an issue where her view [and the
student's] of good practice contradicted agency priorities. The student was
allowed to continue with the case because the supervisor took the matter up
with the agency managers.

The active support of the supervisor here, as in the first case illustration, is
linked to how secure the supervisor is in feeling able to take and manage such
risks.

After discussion of a self-referred marital case, which showed the student's
over-directiveness, the supervisor was asked how things had changed in

supervision since the beginning of the placement. She said '[The student] was prepared to use me, and was prepared to be quite open, but was still quite dependent on expecting me to criticize her work and tell her where she was going wrong . . . now she says things like "I've listened to the tape . . . this is what we might do about it, or I'm not sure, can we talk about it . . ." She takes responsibility for identifying blocks and learning difficulties.'

Although the student is now better able to take responsibility for areas of her own learning, she is still dependent on the supervisor for the validation of this learning, which perhaps reflects Perry's (1970) stage of increased student involvement 'so that we can learn The Answer for ourselves'. The exchange provides further illustrations of concept-leakage in the language which supervisors use to describe students.

The interviewer said, 'You could begin to take risks . . . you have confidence now in her ability to do that, but did you have it before, at the beginning of the placement?' The supervisor said that she had confidence in the student: 'She treats people in a mature way and as equal . . . there are times when the supervision relationship is equal . . . we started out already on the road . . . there have been times when I have felt safe enough to tell her that I'm not sure, and I think that's taking a risk as a practice teacher.'

The researcher asked, 'What have you learnt, how have you developed, during the placement?' The supervisor talked about an occasion when she had 'subcontracted work to a colleague . . . someone had doubts about my capacities, in a specialist team [fostering] . . . I had to come to terms with that . . . There is usually a policy of students not doing this kind of work [fostering] in the agency.'

When asked, 'How does she learn best?' the supervisor replied 'I think like most students do . . . by deciding for herself what she needs to do work on . . . She values feed-back from me but is selective about how she uses it. Of course, there have been times when I've had to push learning points at her, and that's been more difficult.'

The interviewer asked: 'Where are you now, in terms of your development . . . ?' The reply was, 'Well, in group work I'm not an expert and not always confident about students in groups, and I'm very aware of the danger of damage to clients, 'cos I'm not sure the students know enough . . . In the past therefore I have been more directive in my teaching about groups . . . whereas with this student I've been able to take risks and let her get on with it, to make mistakes, and take responsibility for it, without saying do this, this and this . . . it worked better than I could ever have expected.'

The supervisor again demonstrates her increasing ability to take risks, in areas where she does not have expertise, and discovers that it can work well. This supervisor has clearly reached the stage of recognizing that she cannot be an expert, and instructor to the student, in all aspects of social work; and she can allow the student responsibility to select a focus for teaching in the supervision sessions.

However, there is not clear evidence in this interview about whether the supervisor recognizes that she might need to have (or indeed has) a repertoire of teaching approaches to respond to differing student needs. Indeed, the last exchange confirms that she might not be very sure about these differences in the process of learning, and the need not to generalize about *all* or even *most* students, because when asked about how this student learns, the reply is, 'like most students do . . .' The next part of the interview also shows the supervisor's uncertainty about alternative ways to supervise.

> The interviewer said, 'There are a lot of positives which you have de-scribed, in this placement, and it all seems to have worked very well – but what have you got wrong on this placement?' The supervisor said, 'At first, it was [the student's] directiveness – it's the wrong word to use . . . perhaps it's too hard . . . but I wasn't always able to pick it up in a range of ways.' ['For example?'] 'In the child care case . . . [she] was trying to focus on the mother's relationship with her husband, almost trying to persuade her to involve the husband . . . I didn't realize early enough that it was what the student was saying, rather than where the clients had reached . . .' The supervisor was asked, 'How else could you have done it?' She replied 'I don't know, I'm not sure . . .' The researcher asked whether there was anything else the supervisor wished to add that had not been covered. 'Not really, only that there was an amusing bit . . . after this group session when she was so upset after . . . she came and said, "You think I'd learn, wouldn't you?" . . . She felt that she'd got to grips with it [the problem of speaking for people, and urging them to accept her goals rather than their own] in working with individuals and families, but with the group it was like going back in time . . . she was working with the group like it all over again . . . but she could laugh about it too.'
>
> The researcher asked about the difficulty of learning how to use what had been learned in one context in a later, rather different one. The supervisor emphasised that she and the student had talked about the student being 'keen to show that she could transfer skills from one situation and use them in the new situation . . . but that it is not quite as simple as that'.

The importance of being able to transfer learning (in this case from working with families to working in other groups), is the basis of a generic qualification. However, recognizing commonalities and similarities is not enough, because the student was not able to use this understanding in a subsequent piece of practice. The requirement about the transfer of learning between practice in different areas is one which was implemented in 1981, but was poorly under-stood (CCETSW 1984). Some of the lack of understanding seems related to the confusion between the *content* and *process* of learning. Certainly, since *learning* can be a noun or a verb, it can relate both to the *content of what is learned*, as well as to *how that learning occurs.* In this placement, knowing the content of the learning is clearly not sufficient for it to be used in other situations.

The student's conception of learning did not apparently allow her to understand her own involvement in the process of learning, and she still looks to the teacher to play a central role. Clearly in Saljo's terms (1979) she started the placement seeing learning as something which happens to her, rather than as a process of construing meaning for herself. The interview with the student confirms this interpretation.

In the interview with the student, after an introduction about the focus and purpose of the research, the student was asked to describe the placement chronologically.

There had been a pre-placement meeting between student, supervisor and college-based tutor, about the student's learning needs for the placement. She had wanted 'experience in something to do with child care . . . and experience in psychiatric work'. She had considerable previous experience in working with 'the physically handicapped and elderly, so I was trying to get out of that. [The supervisor] thought I should also do some more [of what she had done before] to show how I was doing it differently.

'I was fortunate to get the kind of work I was looking for . . . a fostering assessment, an elderly confused client, and a psychiatric discharge, and groupwork . . . The fostering was an assessment . . . I hadn't done one before . . . [and] there were two marital problems . . . In the first case, I saw the wife who thought the problems were the children . . . I couldn't get husband involved. [In the second one] I got the husband involved sooner, so I learned from my earlier mistake . . . where the husband wouldn't come because he thought I was on the wife's side . . . so I tried to look at how she might cope better . . . [In the latter] I had more a mediator role there . . . identifying things that led to arguments, so they could avoid it again . . . I'd taped the interview . . . I was coming in too quickly, to give them my ideas . . . I went back and started from scratch, it was more basic but more realistic, it was what they could manage . . . both felt at termination that they could come back and ask for help in future . . .'

The interviewer asked, 'What was your task . . . after the formulation of the problem?' The student said that she had 'visited only four times . . . with longer gaps, things were getting better each time . . .'

Much of this discussion was about client groups, and cases. The student described her learning needs in terms of the content of learning, with little attention to the process of her involvement and interaction with her clients. This focus on *content* made the researcher wonder what supervision was like, and whether the interview was a reflection of the supervisory process. The same issue had been evident in the supervisor's interview, so it was decided at the end of the two interviews to ask them whether they would be prepared to tape-record a supervision session and make it available. They agreed, and the material in it strongly supported this assumption.

The interviewer asked about the group, and was told that it was a single parent family group, set up by a student last year. 'There was a core group . . . I raised the possibility of them carrying on after I went, we discussed the possibility of them becoming a Gingerbread group . . . The focus was on financial problems . . . initially they wanted speakers, about supplementary benefit . . . [there was] a lot of lack of self esteem . . . My role was to provide a kind of an overview, and let them talk about what they wanted . . . and allow others to speak . . . Towards the end, I tried to link with other systems, for support and resources, including talking to a local community worker . . .'

It struck the researcher at this point in the interview, because the student seemed to be going into a lot of detail about the work, she perhaps was drawing him into a kind of supervisory role.

Therefore, the researcher asked what the student had learned from this work: 'I got a growth in awareness of their problems . . . when I listened to the tape I was mortified at how much I was speaking, I said so much . . . the next week I was so aware, I tried to say much less . . . [The supervisor] gave me ideas by listening to the tapes and suggesting other things that I could have done . . .' She was asked for an example. 'There were problems of working with an open group . . . I was frustrated that I couldn't involve a new member . . . [the supervisor] gave me special advice . . . She told me that the first week I was the outsider, and the next week, with anyone new, I could say I felt like that last week.'

The student was asked, 'Was that typical of how you used supervision?' She replied, 'Initially, for the first three months, it was process records rather than tapes, it was only tapes after Christmas . . . I did a court report about access in a matrimonial case, I felt I couldn't use tapes . . . after Christmas, it was tapes, mainly with the group . . . usually we had a process record or the tape . . . [At the beginning] she asked me for agenda items for supervision; at first they were mostly hers, but later they were more mine . . .'

The interviewer asked, 'Was there a change of responsibility . . . a change of balance in supervision . . . and were there other changes?' The student said, 'I certainly felt that . . . it carried on and developed . . . from the beginning, they were quite mutual decisions, regarding my work, mutual agreement . . . [The only time it was different] was the fostering assessment [supervised by both the fostering line manager and this supervisor] . . . it was quite good . . . it went well . . . I was able to see what I was doing with the other team leader, but was looking at learning with [this supervisor].'

The change in the pattern of supervision is described from the student's point of view. It had become a more equal relationship, and the student had more responsibility for determining its focus and use.

The researcher asked what was the most important learning on the placement: 'Learning about myself . . . having been unqualified for a long time, you pick up a lot, but I hadn't realized how much I moved too rapidly, in my assessment of a situation . . . I learnt to slow down, and see when the client was ready to move . . . it had never been brought to light before, even in my other placements . . . it came out again and again . . . it came out in retrospect . . . for me that was the big thing, but now at least I know when I do it wrong . . .'

The interviewer said: 'It all seems to have gone very well, but what haven't you learnt, what have you got to do next?' The student said that she 'still could do with more practical experience in child care, I've had a placement in probation and for a long time I worked with the elderly and the handicapped . . . I need more child care still . . . I've learned a lot, I suppose I could have done things better . . . but perhaps one case with a child, especially a child abuse case . . . I really couldn't feel much happier . . .'

During these two interviews, and in the tape-recorded supervision session, there is considerable focus on supervision from an agency-managing point of view, with the supervisor overseeing the student's practice. Where there were shifts in the balance of the relationship, towards a more equal one, it did not seem to accompany a focus on the process of learning in any explicit way. Although there is clear evidence of diversity of approaches to practice, there is little evidence of diversity of approaches to learning.

The shift of balance is towards the student determining the areas in which the supervisor teaches, except where the supervisor recognizes she does not have to be an expert. However, it could be argued that because the learning was still largely content-centred, the student was not able to generalize and transfer the learning from her work with families into the practice of groupwork.

A contribution to the literature shortly after this interview makes clear the distinction between the content and process of learning in supervision, so that learning (both as a noun, and as a verb) can be transferred to less familiar areas, even where the content and context of learning are apparently very different (Gray 1985).

In summary, this placement is characterized by two phases: one where the supervisor was setting the agenda, and the student was dependent on the teacher; the second was where the acknowledgement of lack of expertise by the supervisor went alongside the development of a pattern of more shared responsibility. This is confirmed by the taped supervision of the final assessment session, which has a relaxed tone, with much of the agenda being set and controlled by the student – but with the supervisor confirming or reshaping this as necessary, by maintaining challenges to the student in some areas of her self-assessment.

The next case example has rather fewer positive features.

6.3   Case illustration IV – a new supervisor, and a CSS student

This case illustration is of a placement in a CSS scheme. Only a minority of schemes have placements. During the period in which data were collected CCETSW was reviewing its policies for qualifying training. It was evident that CSS and CQSW training patterns would lead to a single qualification. It was therefore decided to include interviews in the present study from existing CSS placements of this kind. Four such interviews were carried out.

This case illustration demonstrates very limited conceptions of teaching and learning held by the student and the supervisor. It is also included to illustrate some of the difficulties which the researcher faced. It provides a counterpoint to the open and more fluent material reported so far.

Here, a residential worker is undertaking a fieldwork placement in a social services area team. The interviews took place towards the end of the final placement for this student. The objectives had been previously agreed with the study supervisor, whose role is to oversee the student's practice throughout CSS training. For most students, this would include liaison with their line manager, but here (as with other CSS placements) there is a designated supervisor in the office where the student is placed.

> In the interview with the supervisor, she was invited to describe the placement chronologically. She said that CSS placements were different from CQSW courses and contrasted them with her own four year degree CQSW programme which she had completed two years previously. She talked about the student's lack of experience of social work, other than in residential units for children. The placement was intended to give the student experience of working in an area team.
>
> The interviewer asked, 'What does she actually do, on the placement?' The supervisor replied, 'In terms of commitment on my part, it's been quite high. Obviously, with someone like [the student], who's had experience of working with children, but not their families, one couldn't let her loose, so to speak, on families, on her own.'
>
> There were only two cases during the entire placement in which the student had contact with clients – one was a child from a family she had met in her usual work role, prior to the placement. The other case was a family in which she did 'joint work' with the supervisor, 'where she actively participates.' She also joins in office meetings, but the low level of client contact was put down to the difficulty of assigning any cases to her when she was only working in the team on two days a week. 'It is hard to structure work with families on only two days per week.'
>
> There was a discussion about what the student actually does in her two cases. The supervisor said: '[The student] is enthusiastic, and has a lot of ideas . . . [and in her work with the girl in care] she is helping with her weight problem, and helping her to budget to pay back her debts – which she had incurred while she was in the Community Home . . . The case is

really about whether the Care Order should remain in force . . . She spends a lot of time talking to her about the issues, [as I would do, but] . . . it is all a new role for [the student] . . .'

The interviewer asked, 'What do you think she has learnt, on the placement?' 'That it's quite difficult . . . [that] one can only help people if they are prepared to help themselves . . . [and that] being enthusiastic is not enough . . . And the difficulties of being a fieldworker . . . As a residential worker she had always thought that [field] social workers had the easier job, and that she hadn't always understood the decisions of field workers in relation to the children [in her workplace] . . . she would like to be more involved with the families . . .

'Hopefully she's more aware of the complexities of the work we do – that you can't just say "Right, that's the problem, you go and sort it out." She realizes now that there is resistance to making changes. I have the feeling that she feels that sometimes kids go into care because social workers don't try hard enough . . .'

These exchanges show that the supervisor's conception of social work is relatively limited, and the student's conception is even narrower. Such limited views are not easily challenged by the student's involvement in only two cases.

The interview continued with the researcher asking, 'Where does she think that change comes from, then, if it's more complex than just telling them – she has worked [there] for over four years now, she must have some sense about how people change?'

It's quite hard. In the family we are working with together . . . it isn't just the daughter . . . we are trying to restructure the marital relationship.

(*Interviewer*) [Because she doesn't seem to understand, the question is repeated] Residential work has lots of direct care, and containment, and is a rather different role from fieldwork, because you are in such close contact all the time . . . how does she think that change comes about in cases?

I feel that she has been frustrated in residential work by her fellow colleagues – she isn't a typical residential worker – she feels that she should get to know the children [sic].

The supervisor twice does not answer the question about how people change, and throughout seems too unclear about the purpose of social work practice. The supervisor has, however, internalized the classical supervision model (perhaps from her own student experience) and uses pathological notions in describing the student:

One of [her] problems . . . is her challenging personality . . . she needs to make it less challenging, so she can take people with her, instead of getting their backs up, or alienating them. I haven't discussed it much with her . . . I'd like to discuss it with her . . . I've touched on it . . . She is like that with [my colleagues] . . . I was on leave for a week, and one of the team was doing a Section, a compulsory admission to psychiatric hospital, which the student challenged. The social worker involved gave her all the answers . . . but another social worker became quite angry at [the student] doing this . . . the student felt that it was part of her student role to be questioning . . . [but] social work decisions are usually hard . . . you have to balance things . . . it was a bit worrying . . .

(*Interviewer*) . . . Is it *how* she asks the questions that is the problem? ['Yes, yes.'] Does it have any impact on her work with her clients?

I think it could do, with certain families . . . in one case she knew the girl, in the other, I had already established trust . . . [This student] going in cold to a family . . . she could make them feel sagging. I feel she could become too familiar too quickly and this tends to put people off.

(*Interviewer*) Sometimes, in social work, people need to be given space . . .

Yes, I think one of the problems I have had with [this student] is in terms of privacy, as a person . . . she tends to pass barriers . . . [she] asks direct questions about my private life . . . and of others . . . An illustration was this interview . . . [She asked] where did I know you from . . . via [her colleague]. Then she asked how·did [the colleague] meet you. I thought it was irrelevant.

It appears that the supervisor finds the student quite a problem, but does not feel able to challenge her over-intrusiveness. The interviewer asks about assessment, and the structural problems CSS presents for the supervisor, especially for new supervisors.

Well . . . I've been in a stressful period myself . . . I'm trying to decide if it's from work, or having a very demanding student . . . Yes, I'd be quite concerned – I think she needs to change. I'm willing to say that to her tutor. [Clarification confirms that she means the study supervisor] . . . I can't recommend pass/fail . . . I can do a report, if I want to . . . it's not expected . . . One has a certain amount of concern, because I'm sure the problems I've encountered, with [this student] others have . . . In three weeks' time she'll have gone [she sounds relieved at the prospect].

(*Interviewer*) Do you have contact with the study supervisor?

It's a bit difficult . . . [her only connection with the agency and the course is with this one student] . . . we were going to work out objectives [for the placement,] but then they were worked out by [the student] and the study supervisor.

(*Interviewer*) What have you learnt about supervision, yourself?

I haven't really structured particular times . . . we're together most of the day . . . She's got such a lot of ideas of her own, which makes it quite hard for her to listen to other people [sic].

(*Interviewer*) That must make being the supervisor quite difficult?

She's not an easy student. I don't get much from her, she always seems to know already . . . She had a traumatic life [of her own], like some of the stuff in a social services file . . . [Sighs] She needs to be challenged . . . I'd very much like to say she needs another placement, toning down her approach, but whether I have the strength – I'd personally find it very difficult . . .

(*Interviewer*) If there are no clear guidelines for assessment, that makes it very difficult. Is there any way you could get support from the study supervisor? . . . [if you are not sure that] this is the level for a qualified worker?

I think she has some quite good ideas . . . [but] they need to be trained in the right way . . . [but] it could be totally disastrous if one tried to impose from authority [the student is Deputy Head of the Unit] one's personal belief that everybody else isn't doing a very good job, and should be doing it like [her] . . . She's going back to [her own work-place] now.

(*Interviewer*) Could you write to her new supervisor there, with the information that you wished you'd had at the beginning of the placement?

mmm . . . mmm . . . [uncertainly] In my relationship with [the student], I feel ambivalent about her . . . it's difficult, one has to have a reasonable relationship, especially the amount of contact I have with her. We're together for two full days every week . . .

(*Interviewer*) It must be pretty exhausting.

It is. It is . . . She finds it hard to sit and read, she has to be doing something . . . she doesn't take account of the pressures on me, and she's just another one . . . normally, in CQSW placements they have a caseload, they go out, at least they [supervisor and student] can have a break from each other . . . [After a rounding off to the interview] I think I should go home and have a nice rest. I hope all this is useful to you.

The lack of support for this supervisor (compounded by the structure of the CSS scheme), and her isolation from the study supervisor are matters of concern. This supervisor also thinks that there is a right way to work, and the student's ideas need 'to be trained in the right way.' There is further evidence of the classical model in supervision, and of reproductive conceptions of teaching and learning in this placement. There is perhaps reason for concern about the student's rather directive approach to practice since she passed the placement and course, and is now qualified.

In reading this account, and listening to the tape a number of times, it is evident that in this particular interview, the convention which has been generally adopted (i.e. deleting 'ums' and 'ers' to tidy up the exchanges) has minimized the uncertainty and hesitancy of the supervisor. Many of her sentences are interspersed with 'sort of', and she interjects the word 'hopefully' into a number of her replies, especially about the student. The tentativeness and passivity of the supervisor, and her not pursuing meetings with the study supervisor, are reflected in the flat tone to the interview.

The interview with the student was even more difficult. It was the most awkward, and least satisfactory of the entire study. Just before the tape was switched on the student said she did not understand the learning styles exercise, so she didn't do it, and 'anyway the animals had such funny names' she didn't see how it would help her to learn. The interviewer explained that it wasn't intended to help her to learn, but to give an indication of *how* she approached the task. She said that she had just played with the cards (for almost an hour). She seemed offhand, and casual to the point of rudeness.

> [The interview began with another statement about the purpose of the research, and its focus on how people learn, rather than just on what they learn.] The student said: 'I've had lots of supervisors in the past but they have never made it clear what or how to learn.'
>
> She described the purpose of the placement in very general terms, which sounded as though she were reading out guidelines. The tone of voice seemed to indicate surprise that anyone should ask, and that I should know already. She was asked for an example.
>
> The initial objective that I had to do [sic] was to look at the intake and referral team, and weigh up the pros and cons, and do some written work . . . Intake teams are necessary, efficient and work well together as a team [sic] . . . they deal with the referrals . . . they decide that it is a long or relatively short term problem . . . a minimum of three months to a year maximum.
>
> (*Interviewer*) How do they judge it, then?
>
> I've got the criteria that they use. They are upstairs – you should have said if you wanted them . . . There is a list of six points, six objectives.
>
> (*Interviewer*) Don't you still have to make judgements, though?
>
> It is difficult, for example, 'Is the family motivated to work with us?' . . . They may not even recognize they have a problem.

This early part of the interview shows that the student was surprised that the interviewer did not know what the purpose of the placement was, and then described social work in somewhat simplistic terms. She was asked what she had learnt on the placement, and described social work in crude behavioural terms:

> They work quite closely with the families, but very often, you're only in an advisory capacity, not a very practical capacity, so you can only offer so much help or advice on how you feel they should be carrying out certain things within the family structure . . . If you can't be of any practical assistance, I think very often it is very difficult – they [clients] say yes, yes, to you, and then don't do anything once the door is closed behind you.

There are cases where you can give a bit of practical help to the family, then they are motivated to change or be helped.

(*Interviewer*) Practical help? Can you give me an example?

'A woman lost the wheel from her pram and rang the office. The duty social worker went to town to fix it . . . that was quite good.'

(*Interviewer*) Do social workers give any other kinds of help besides advice?

Sometimes you have to work in a sort of family therapy situation . . . trying to work out the relationships within the family.

(*Interviewer*) How do you think they do this?

Well there are varying techniques, really, some people do it with intense interviews, and family sessions with all the family together. Other people interview the clients separately and try to get them to talk about their problems.

(*Interviewer*) What exactly do they do, in these interviews?

You try and work out what is the position of the problem in the family and how each of them can cope with it . . .

(*Interviewer*) OK, so that's a kind of diagnosis, or plan . . . how do you get to change what is going on?

[pause] . . . By making alternative suggestions like a bit of give and take. [This is said in a tone which seems incredulous that anyone didn't know how to do it.]

(*Interviewer*) For example?

If a child is truanting from school, and the reason is in the family, you make out some kind of incentive for the child to go to school, perhaps for reward to come from the mother . . . it needs a bit of give and take on both sides really.

(*Interviewer*) Is that the kind of thing you did in your residential work?

It was in a Community Home.

(*Interviewer*) What kinds of things were you doing?

It varies, from general basic caring needs, right through to individual counselling or therapy. [This feels like a lecture, about 'What goes on . . .' rather than 'what *she* did'.] In my experience, if there is a problem, you tell them what the problem is and try to get them to solve the problem by a sort of reward system. If they do something then they get something for doing it.

(*Interviewer*) Is this how to do it for all clients?

No, for some it is worthwhile to sit and chat with them to find out how they feel about something. For children, though, you need a practical approach to their behaviour.

(*Interviewer*) If there was a child in the Home, what would you do, if the child was in care?

There was a good instance last year, there was a girl who ran off with her boyfriend; he lived next door, he was married with three kids. They ran off to London together. Her parents reported them missing . . . They were picked up in London, [caught] shoplifting. She was received into care under a place of safety, for her moral safety was what they called it. They tried to charge him with unlawful sexual intercourse. She was in care for 28 days, so we tried to work with a contract for the individual and the family . . . It only took two to three days to realize there was an absolute breakdown in the relationship between the parents and child which initiated her running away from home. We worked on this contract for 28 days. Just before the 28 days, the parents decided they weren't quite ready to have her home . . . because there were certain areas that were still untouched by the work . . . There was two months intensive work, the residential workers went round to the family at the weekends, and if there were problems, they would sort them out.

(*Interviewer*) On this placement, tell me a bit about your work.

We have been working towards revoking the Care Order. With the client I knew, the family have always had money problems, so I thought I would work with [the daughter] to help her pay her debts off . . . I'm succeeding, but it's a very slow progress compared to residential work . . . You are in a stronger position, [in residential work] to do something about it . . . you can't control them as much in fieldwork. You have to entice her or encourage her . . .

This model of practice is to do primarily with authority and instruction of clients, backed up by behavioural reinforcements. She sees two possibilities for intervening – practical help (which she values) and 'chat with them to find out how they feel about something'.

There are many examples in this interview of the student answering questions at a level of generality, rather than about her own views or experiences, which was disconcerting. She also seemed to use words in not very precise ways, for example. 'The initial objective that I had to do . . .'

There was an interruption here, with someone asking, 'Is that your car in the way?' to which the student replied in an offhand way, 'Oh I expect so, yes, is it a [make of car]?' 'Yes.' The student went to move her car and the tape was turned over. There are about ten minutes more of the interview. However, the recording did not come out at all.

In the interview, the student was domineering, didn't always seem to listen to the questions, and seemed offhand. She treated the researcher at some points as though he knew nothing about social work. At other times she seemed incredulous that I should ask questions when there was obviously a (single) right answer. Indeed, another research interview had already been undertaken in that office, which she knew about. I felt very angry at the end of the interview; she was causing a good deal of distress to her supervisor, as well as creating problems in the office.

When, at the end of her interview, she was offered the routine three-way discussion with her supervisor, she stayed for a few minutes only, and seemed bored by the discussion. She went off 'to do some shopping', despite earlier having agreed to join the supervisor and researcher for lunch.

This chapter has gone into detail about some aspects of supervision, and events in the placement which determined approaches to supervision. In these case illustrations, it is intended to get at the meanings supervisors and students attached to the subtleties and nuances of teaching and learning. All of the placements in this part of the research could have been included, but the selection given indicates the kind and range of data collected, and gives the material necessary to begin to develop a grounded model of learning in supervision.

7

Towards a Model of Learning in Professional Education

7.1   Making patterns and making sense

At the beginning of the book, the descriptions and explanations of teaching and learning in supervision were shown to be rooted in the classical literature. The data collected have demonstrated the persistent influence of that model (with its emphasis on teaching, and what was to be taught) sometimes to the detriment of students' learning.

The adult learning research literature demonstrated that it was possible (and indeed desirable) to focus research attention on the approaches to teaching and learning which students and supervisors use, and some of the factors which might affect those choices.

In this study, of learning within natural learning environments (which in social work is a complex mixture of intellectual, affective and value-based learning tasks), the data represent a level of detail and focus which can describe teaching and learning processes from the perspective of those who were directly involved.

Earlier, it was suggested that this study should produce descriptions of supervision sessions, and accounts of the interpretations and meanings those involved attached to their experiences. The recognition of what was salient in the accounts, and identifying patterns, explanations and interpretations with those involved would also be required. These things have now been accomplished in the selection, presentation and interpretation of the data, so the steps of developing those generalizations into a model of teaching and learning, and providing some basis for future policy development, can now be addressed.

Initially, the focus of the study had been on the effect of match or mis-match of teaching styles and learning styles, which suggested that it might be possible to develop a schematic typology of teachers and learners, and to explore the impact of match and mis-match.

The matrix in Figure 1 shows that in Boxes A and D, 'fit' or 'match' of styles occurs, whilst in Boxes B and C styles are mis-matched. The questionnaire responses confirmed that supervisors had difficulty in supervising those students who did not learn in the way supervisors were expecting to teach – and

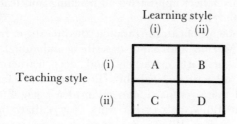

Figure 1   A teaching and learning styles matrix

Figure 2   A learning style and stage matrix

	Stage I	Stage II	Stage III
Surface/serialist approach	A	B	C
Deep/holist approach	D	E	F

that supervisors preferred to teach students who had learnt like they themselves had, in a significant learning experience.

What became clear, in trying to assign responses to the matrix in Figure 1, was that some supervisors changed their approach through time, or with different students. An element of 'stage' was needed, so the model was refined during the collection of data in the single case study. Figure 2 reflects stages of development for teachers and learners – thus it would be possible to consider a match or mis-match by superimposing a matrix for a student onto that for a supervisor.

This revised matrix also caused difficulties – the boundaries between the stages were unclear, so that whilst some supervisors could readily be assigned (e.g. Box B) others might have been on a boundary (e.g. between A and B) whilst yet others could be in more than one Box (e.g. B and E) during a single placement. These early attempts at classification were premature and, with hindsight, can be seen to have been devised as a conceptual frame *into which data could be fitted*.

The framework had not been built around and from the data, so the model was a simplistic attempt to theorize. Elton and Laurillard (1979) show that it is not theories (with hypotheses to test against data), but models that are needed:

> A theory, by its very nature, explains all phenomena within its region of applicability; hence a theory of learning should be relevant and valid, whenever learning takes place. A model interprets rather than explains, and whether it is applicable to a particular learning situation can only be verified by testing the model against the situation in each instance.

There was, however, one important outcome from these preliminary attempts to systematize the data. It became evident that teachers and learners could be assigned to more than one place, so any categorization could not be a typology of individuals; it could only reflect approaches to teaching and learning in the context of a particular placement.

There are similar problems of categorization in the literature. In describing the work of Pask, or Marton and Saljo, describing individual subjects as 'serialists' and 'holists', or 'surface learners' and 'deep learners' should be avoided, although not all writers heed this (Entwistle and Hanley 1977). Laurillard (1978), and more recent studies (Ramsden 1979; Entwistle and Ramsden 1983) confirm Entwistle's earlier work (1977) that approaches to learning are context-dependent. What is described, then, are approaches used in particular learning contexts.

Furthermore, a matrix of style against stage would only allow the plotting of positions for supervisors, or for students – it would not necessarily explain *the patterns of interaction between them*. It is necessary to identify the kinds of patterns of interaction found, and to build them into an interactive model. To do this, some of the main features of the case illustrations are reiterated, to make building blocks which can then be combined into a unifying conceptual framework.

7.2   Building blocks for an interactive model of teaching and learning in supervision

In some case examples, teaching and learning valued the contribution of the teacher, and what was to be taught. There was a focus on the *content* of learning. This pattern seemed to be associated with an expectation that there is a single, right way to practise, and that there is a single right way to teach and learn. Such a position also involves a clearly hierarchical relationship between teacher and learner, and locates responsibility for assessment largely with the teacher, who has authority derived from expertise. This pattern (or expectation of it) is a *Level One* interaction.

Other examples of teaching and learning interactions saw students' contributions to learning as central. There was some attention given to the *process* of learning. What students bring to the placement, and to supervision, was seen as important, and they had an active role in constructing meaning from their own experiences. There was a recognition of diversity – in approaches to teaching, learning and practice. This pattern (or expectation of it) is a *Level Two* interaction.

In some instances supervisors not only recognized that all students may not learn in the same way, or that the same student might learn things in different ways at different times, but they also showed that they could teach in different ways. Equally, some students recognized the need to use different approaches for different learning tasks and contexts, and showed them during the placement. This position is associated with diversity in the range of client problems dealt with, and with versatility of intervention strategies. This pattern (or expectation of it) is a *Level Three* interaction.

There were instances of changing patterns in supervision, showing movement between these levels; and there were some problems where expectations of supervision were at different levels. These complexities will be considered after articulating the features of the three patterns of interaction to show that they reflect qualitatively different levels of interaction in supervision. The detail of the process of model-building, and the way the following features were derived from the data have been reported elsewhere (Gardiner 1987c) so they are presented here in summary.

7.2.1 Level One – a focus on the CONTENT of learning

Some of the features of *Level One* sketched above (especially the focus on the content of learning, and the expectation of passive learning) can be illustrated fully from the data gathered throughout the study. The first and third autobiographical experiences demonstrated the influence of the classical model. In them, supervisors believed that the right way to supervise was to reflect the hierarchical casework relationship with clients, and to maintain control not only of what the student should be learning, but also of the single right path to achieve it.

The single case study also provided evidence of *Level One* interactions, because the supervisor was concerned to demonstrate her teaching, and often involved the student in detailed rehearsals so that he could learn the right way to practise. Her doubts about the student's performance encouraged her into more directive teaching. The student seemed cue-conscious (Miller and Parlett 1973) and was passive during these parts of supervision sessions. The student conceived of his learning task (with this supervisor, at that point in the placement) as reproductive, passive learning. The supervisor confirmed this in her mid-way evaluation:

> [He] like all students, is anxious to pass and has been conscious of his assessment . . . He admits he saw fieldwork as a way of distancing himself from his 'total' experience of residential work . . . The distancing and concern about his assessment has shown in most aspects of his early work. His first recordings were factual, minimal with little indication of his involvement . . . Similarly, in supervision he has tended to talk about his cases rather formally which has not made it easy to judge where he is in relation to the client . . .

In the questionnaire exercise, *Level One* interactions were also much in evidence, with references to traditional patterns of teaching and learning, and of concept-leakage in the pathologizing of students. One supervisor used that terminology to refer to her own failings as a learner. There were also references to apprenticeship models of supervision, which illustrate an expectation that the right way to practise can be learnt by watching others. It is evident that the classical supervision literature is founded on assumptions which reflect *Level One* in this framework.

In the case illustrations, there are further examples of *Level One* patterns. The experienced supervisor with a failing student (Case Illustration II) exemplifies many of the features of this position, with his belief in a single, right way to teach and learn, and a preoccupation with individualized, sequential teaching. He found it difficult to conceive of others contributing to the teaching, in a team, and held a very traditional view about social work practice. This example showed the powerful constraining effect such limited conceptions of the learning process can have on student learning and the supervisory relationship.

The CSS placement (Case Illustration IV) shows a heavy reliance on observation, and apprenticeship models, with the student literally sitting by her supervisor for two days a week. Neither appeared to expect the student to be actively involved in her own learning, and they had not arranged supervision sessions as discrete entities, where they might reflect on the student's experience.

In the major case example (Case Illustration I) there were *Level One* interactions where the supervisor felt that the student's understanding of social work was at a very generalized level, and that he needed more specificity and some direct teaching. Whilst for some supervisors *Level One* reflects the stage they have reached in conceptualizing learning, and their role as teachers (like the specialist supervisor with the failing student), for others it is a stage they are moving from (the supervisors in the single case study and in Case Illustration III), and for yet others it is a pattern they will adopt in response to their analysis of the student's competence and his learning needs at that point (Case I). Clearly, *Level One* interactions can be appropriate and functional, when the learning task, and the context of learning demand passive, reproductive learning.

7.2.2   *Level Two – a focus on the PROCESS of learning*

The features of *Level Two* described earlier (with a recognition of diversity, and a focus on the active involvement of the learner in the learning process) can also be illustrated more fully from the data reported here. The Göteborg work might characterize this level as demonstrating a shift from reproductive to constructive conceptions of learning (i.e. from surface to deep strategies). One can hypothesize that deep learning outcomes in social work education are unlikely if the interactive patterns do not reflect at least this level of understanding of learning.

The second autobiographical experience showed the supervisor recognizing that supervisors taught, and students learned, in different ways. The questionnaire exercise generated considerable evidence of this level of interaction, in terms of supervisors acknowledging that they do not need to be an expert, or that students had responsibility for their own learning. The questionnaire was also important in helping to distinguish Levels One and Two by the ability to distinguish the content and process of learning, through the answers to the 'what' and 'how' questions. Those with limited reproductive conceptions of learning did not differentiate between, or confused, what had been learnt with how it had been learnt.

In the single case study, *Level Two* interactions were evident towards the end of the placement, especially after the student had acknowledged greater involvement in his client-work and after some good self-evaluations for supervision. In the main case illustration (Case I), much of the placement after the death of a colleague in the office showed the student demonstrating that he could take responsibility for – and involvement in – his learning, in his relationship with his supervisor and the rest of the team, and in his cases.

In Case Illustration III there was also evidence of *Level Two* patterns. As the placement developed, the student took increasing responsibility for setting the agenda for supervision, and for assessing her own work and learning. The supervisor in that example showed that she was increasingly able to take risks in supporting the student's work, even when she herself did not have content-expertise (in groupwork, and in fostering).

The value of this level of interaction, and of the reflective process in construing meaning for oneself has been long recognized, even if it does not always characterize social work supervision (Watts 1810; in Entwistle and Hanley, 1977):

> It is meditation and study that transfers and conveys the notions and sentiments of others to ourselves, so as to make them properly our own. It is our judgement on them, as well as our memory of them, that makes them become our own property . . .

7.2.3 Level Three – META-LEARNING and the demonstration of versatility

The identifying feature of this level is the recognition *and* demonstration of versatility in approaches to teaching and learning. It includes students and supervisors using their own learning processes as the basis (content) of further learning (process) of a higher order. This meta-learning, or learning to learn, can promote transfer of the content *and* process of learning to contexts other than those in which the original learning arose.

Only a few students and supervisors in the study demonstrated this kind of interaction. It is possible that some teachers and students had not reached this level of learning conception, but for others it may be that contextual factors (e.g. a college/agency milieu; or teaching and assessment methods which did not value such learning) constrained them from use even though an individual may have been capable of them. The questionnaire exercise showed that some supervisors realized the need for a repertoire of approaches to teaching, to meet differing learning needs of students, and a few indicated that they made such changes.

Case Illustration I showed that the supervisor was able to use her understanding of the learning process in determining her initial response to the student. She demonstrated later that she could encourage and tolerate more freedom for the student, and a more active role for him, which was reinforced by the crisis following the death in the office. She went on to distinguish his strengths and weaknesses in component parts of the learning process, so that she could give particular attention both to the student's ability to generalize from particular experiences, and his ability to be more specific in the application of his generalized understandings.

In doing so she demonstrated that she recognized, and could act on, the twin elements (of generalizing from particular experiences, and the subsequent application of those generalizations in new and different practice areas) as essential elements in developing the capacity to transfer learning (Gardiner 1986a). Biggs (1985) calls these higher order processes 'meta-learning'. In Case I, the student's understanding of these elements of the learning process was demonstrated by his comments to the researcher in the three way discussion about the need to establish what was salient in any given experience as the basis of recognizing patterns which can be generalized.

The transfer of learning is at the heart of generic social work training, because students cannot rehearse in training all of the types of work which they will be required to undertake in their professional career. A selection of learning experiences must be made, together with helping the student to develop the ability to generalize from them, and to judge later whether these generalizations are of value in new and different situations.

The only instance in the study where both student and supervisor appeared to begin the placement with *Level Three* interactions was where the supervisor was an experienced team leader (but who had supervised very few students), and the student was an experienced, bright student in her final placement. Their initial sessions established a contract which allowed the student to demonstrate her competence in a variety of interventions. In supervision, she was able to show that she understood the distinction between reproductive learning and deeper, constructive learning. Sometimes she asked for help to find out more about a case she had encountered, which the supervisor offered, or she followed it up herself in private study. The example she described in her interview concerned working with a depressed young mother. She followed up her initial contacts by asking for help in supervision about working with depressed people, then read widely about depression. As more of her caseload also reflected problems of depression in a very deprived community she eventually wrote a project essay for college on the subject.

Her supervisor was able to offer some direct input, but also to involve her with other professionals who were more experienced in the work than him. However, in relation to other kinds of work in her workload he offered a combination of direct teaching, and help in reflection with her on her learning from the work, and the development of her learning during the rest of the course. They shared responsibility for producing the final placement assessment report. The pattern of their final few supervision sessions was described as 'consultation' by which they meant the student took the initiative in determining the amount and nature of their contact (not always in formal sessions), and the nature and focus of discussions in supervision. The experience of supervising a range of staff over a period had clearly given this supervisor the experience to recognize both the need for diversity and autonomy in learning – although this was the first student placement where he had been able to act in this way.

That placement, like some others described above, shows the importance of the supervisor valuing team teaching as part of a repertoire of approaches. The direct involvement of the team in which the student was placed came up in a number of the interviews, but not always with a clear recognition of the contribution which others could make. However, where there is some involvement of other team members (or others outside who contribute to a teaching team), it is necessary to distinguish between passing on the student to another, alternative expert (a Level One pattern) and encouraging the student to contribute reciprocally to the team, using others differentially to offer a range of teaching-learning experiences.

There are other ways to recognize *Level Three* interactions – meta-learning involves the ability to distinguish various orders of communication (meta-communication) and to ascribe accurate meaning to communications. In the practice domain, the work of Bateson *et al.* (1956) was an important contribution to working with families and groups who were unable to distinguish (or who deliberately confused) orders and levels of communication.

When, in the study, an interviewee asks 'Is this what you want me to talk about?' and 'What do you mean by that?' or 'Is it OK to carry on in this way?' this may be evidence of the ability to look at different levels of communication, and discriminate the level of the interaction. This was well demonstrated between supervisor, student and researcher in the three-way feedback interview in Case Illustration I.

No doubt other studies are required, of a longitudinal nature, with a larger (perhaps more stratified) sample before being sure about the proportions of supervisors who could work with students in this way. Equally, staff development programmes for supervisors would need to ensure that the promotion of meta-learning was seen as a legitimate (and central) part of the supervisory process in placements.

7.3 Towards a new model of learning in supervision

The three levels of teaching and learning interaction found in the data can be synthesized into a model which describes and explains some features of supervisory relationships. The kinds of developmental changes described by Perry (1970), and by Saljo (1979), and changes seen during placements, show that the three patterns of interaction can be considered as parts of a developmental continuum. This allows an explicit statement of the qualitative changes in conceptions of learning which characterize these positions. The three stage model is one which shows the three levels of interaction as ideal-types, arising from a match of stages of conception of learning held by students and supervisors.

STAGE ONE is a surface-reproductive conception of learning, characterized by a predominant focus on the content of what is to be taught and learnt (i.e. facts or procedures). It will be associated with an expectation that teaching-learning patterns in supervision will be hierarchical, and value the contribution of the expert-teacher rather than the learner. Such a learning conception is likely to constrain supervision to Level One interactions only.

The second stage is characterized by learning of a qualitatively different order. Learning is construed as an active search for meaning by the student. Others may help to learn, but they cannot teach them all they need to learn, because significant learning arises from the learner reflecting on the meaning of experiences. *This deeper conception of learning (STAGE TWO) is characterized by a focus on the process of learning (i.e. an active-constructive search for meaning from experience).*

Just as these first two stages are qualitatively different orders of conception, so too is the third level. Whilst Stage Two represents an ability to focus on the process of learning, and not simply on the content of learning, Stage Three represents a further transformation, of learning from learning experiences through reflection on the process of learning. It comprises identifying different approaches to teaching and learning; and accurately discriminating learning approaches required by a range of tasks in different contexts. This third order conception of learning is what Biggs (1985) calls 'meta-learning'. This kind of learning-to-learn is not simply about improving the effectiveness of learning at lower levels. Here it is specifically used to describe a higher order reflection process, concerning one's differential approaches to learning in a range of learning tasks, in a range of learning contexts. *STAGE THREE conceptions of learning are characterized by a focus on meta-learning, and learning to learn* (i.e. being able to use and evaluate qualitatively different approaches for different learning tasks).

It should be noted that in this scheme, each higher level conception of learning subsumes lower level conceptions. Thus, a Stage Two conception of learning (of active involvement of the learner, allowing the use of deep strategies) encompasses the possibility of also using surface-reproductive strategies for some learning tasks. In other words, if student and supervisor hold Stage Two conceptions of learning, it is possible for them to exhibit both Level One *and* Level Two patterns of interaction.

This model allows the demonstrated patterns of interaction in supervision to be seen as the outcomes of the conceptions of learning held by students and supervisors. It is possible for individuals to move to higher stage conceptions, and extend the range of possible interactions in which they can engage. The research into adult learning in higher education, and the present study, both point to the context-dependence of the chosen strategy for a particular learning task.

Therefore demonstrated patterns of interaction will be the result of teachers' and learners' perceptions of the requirements of specific tasks, operating within the constraints of the highest stage of conception of learning they have reached.

These features can be represented schematically. Figure 3 shows the final model which is derived from the data in this study.

Figure 3   A model of teaching and learning interactions

Conceptions of learning

	Stage I	Stage II	Stage III
Teachers' conceptions	T_1	T_2	T_3
LEVELS OF INTERACTION	LEVEL I	LEVEL II	LEVEL III
Students' conceptions	S_1	S_2	S_3

Illustrations from the case examples demonstrate the use of this model. In Case Illustration I, in Chapter 5, the supervisor had a mature Stage Three conception of learning (T_3) at the beginning of the placement. This enabled her to select some teaching strategies to provide Level One interactions with the student, who had begun with Stage One passive, reproductive conceptions of learning (S_1). They later moved to Level Two interactions, with the student taking much more responsibility for his learning (through developing a constructive conception of learning – S_2), and the supervisor helping him to make sense of, and generalize from, his experiences.

It is now possible to return to the question of *match and mis-match of approaches to learning* in the light of the model. Clearly, using the level of conception of learning as the criterion to distinguish the developmental or stage dimension of the model makes it much easier to explain the effects of mis-matched approaches to teaching and learning.

Matching can produce the three ideal-type interactive patterns (Levels One, Two and Three). *The effect of mis-matching, though, is dependent on the level at which the mis-match occurs.* Thus, if a student has a Level Two conception of learning (S_2) whilst the supervisor has a Level One conception (T_1) some choices appear to be open. The student can change to a Stage One approach, taking a more passive role, letting his teacher take responsibility for the teaching and learning (producing Level One interactive patterns, as in the single case study). Alternatively, the student could persist with Stage Two approaches and risk problems in the supervisory relationship, perhaps even risking failure (as the student in Case Illustration II may have done).

Certainly the researcher's own experience as a supervisor is clarified by this model. Early placements saw him emphasizing a teaching role (T_1), but, fortunately, some of the students seemed versatile (S_3), and able to adapt to that approach. Their higher level conceptions allowed them to use different strategies in other parts of the course; and, later, in the placement, as the supervisor's approaches to teaching developed (to T3).

Case Illustration I showed a supervisor whose conception of learning was Stage Three, which allowed her to select approaches to respond to the learning needs of the student – initially for a Level One interaction, before later guiding him in a paradigm shift to Level Two. Case II, by contrast, shows the constraining influence on the student's learning of a Level One conception of learning held by the supervisor.

If both teacher and learner have Stage Three conceptions, but they encounter a mis-match of approaches between them, then it would be possible to discuss the requirements of the particular learning task, and make any necessary adjustments to their approaches. The effect of mis-match of approaches to learning is therefore a direct consequence of the level of learning conception. The biggest problems found in this research seemed to arise from students or supervisors (especially the latter) having Stage One conceptions of learning, and assuming that there are single right ways to teach, learn and assess (i.e. Level One interactions).

This finding may be generally true in higher education, but it is a particular problem in social work for two reasons: first, the classical model of supervision reinforces Level One interactions; second, most supervisors are relatively inexperienced and irregular teachers, so they may be constrained from developing their conceptions of teaching and learning.

Whilst this research was being undertaken, and the study was being written up, other research findings were reported in the literature. The present study is illuminative, and derived from a small sample, therefore it is useful to consider whether the findings and the model are congruent with more substantial research elsewhere.

7.4   The model and other recent work

The earlier review of research on adult learning, in Chapter 4, covered the work available at the beginning of the study. Other work has been published since, and it is considered here to put the present findings and model into a wider context. It is worth emphasizing that the distinctions between deep and surface learning, and their relation to conceptions of learning, have been extended and replicated in Sweden, Holland, Australia and England. Studies in English Universities have shown, through correlational and factor analyses, that personality traits are associated with comprehension or operation styles of learning; and that a deep approach involves the ability to think logically and flexibly, combined with the personality characteristics 'sceptical intellectual autonomy' (Entwistle and Ramsden 1983). In Australia, Biggs (1985) confirms the relation of intelligence to deep approaches, and 'below a certain level of ability, the factor structure disintegrates' (Entwistle 1987). Saljo (1987) says:

It has become evident that there is a functional relationship between the mode in which people subjectively construe learning and the way they go about dealing with learning tasks . . . An absolutist conception of learning (and knowledge) has been found to be associated with . . . a surface approach.

Of particular interest is work in Holland (Van Rossum, Deijkers and Hamer, 1985; Van Rossum and Schenk 1984) which confirmed the Swedish findings of qualitatively different levels of conception of learning. Their work also relates the conceptions of learning to associated concepts like teaching, understanding and insight, the application of knowledge, and the distinction between active and passive learning. Van Rossum shows that the various levels of conception directly affect how these related ideas are seen, in qualitatively different ways. Learning conceptions, study strategies and learning outcomes are also shown by their work to be closely related.

Whilst that work confirms the basic distinction between Stages One and Two in the model presented here, it is necessary to look at other work for Stage Three conceptions and Level Three interactions. Van Rossum has reported identifying a sixth conception: 'learning seen as self-realisation' which is similar to what Biggs (1985) describes as meta-learning: 'the rather specialized application of metacognition to the area of student learning', and to Flavell's definition of meta-cognitive processes (1976):

> . . . one's knowledge concerning one's own cognitive processes and products . . . (and) the active monitoring and consequent regulation of those processes in relation to the cognitive objects or data on which they bear.

Biggs' work confirms meta-cognition as a higher-order construct, and as such it is in essence what we have elsewhere called 'learning to learn' (Gardiner 1984a):

> The ability to do this is what I mean by 'learning to learn' since it involves the recognition of one's own learning processes, and the ability to modify them.

The regulation of the validating body, that students demonstrate the ability to transfer learning from one area of practice to another requires just such skills. Gardiner (1984b) has also defined the elements of the learning process which make up such a transfer:

> In other words, the learning process is about changes in the way we see, and make sense of, the world . . . By the 'transfer of learning' I mean those parts of the overall learning process which I have described in detail above – i.e. having an experience, recognising what is salient, the building up of patterns, making patterns of the patterns which become generalisations, and then the recognition in new situations that the earlier generalisations may be appropriate or relevant. Thus, both generalisations derived from particular experiences *and* the application of these generalisations are essential components of the transfer of learning.

This view of learning, as changes in the way we see and make sense of the world, is indicative of the focus of this study itself, in its focus upon the ways students and supervisors construe their world. Saljo (1987) discusses precisely these issues as a focus for study, shifting attention away from mental mechanisms and information-processing models, towards people's conceptions of reality. He quotes Goodman (1978) about this complementary line of research being guided by:

> simply this: never mind mind, essence is not essential, and matter doesn't matter. We do better to focus on versions than worlds.

In considering how to intervene, to improve learning in the future Saljo says:

> Our basis for intervention will lie in our knowledge about what constitutes learning problems in our particular field . . . In other words it will be about how people succeed in expanding their intellectual repertoires to encompass new and previously unseen 'ways of worldmaking'.

The present study, whilst illustrative and illuminative in professional education, is clearly congruent with lines of enquiry which (at the time the data were collected and the development of the model was in process) were not known to the present author.

The publication of work in progress from this study triggered responses in the literature. The distinction between content and process of learning (i.e. the distinction between Stage One and Stage Two conceptions of learning) and the need to consider both, was not one with which some teachers were comfortable. Whittington (1986) in a review of the literature prompted by this work says:

> [Badger] also notes that the concept of transfer lends itself to a preoccupation with process and is concerned that the content implications of transfer might be neglected . . . Jenny Gray has no such concern. She argues from personal experience that the preoccupation with process is highly functional and that the degree of importance of the learning process over the original learning content varies in relation to the degree of difference between practice contexts: the larger the difference between contexts, the more important the learning process is in assisting social workers to practise competently.

Because Stage Three conceptions of learning are at the core of the debate on the transfer of learning, and developing learning-to-learn competence, some recent work on the transfer of learning was reviewed.

Traditionally, it is held that transfer is difficult to demonstrate, especially outside the discipline or domain of the original learning. Wollman (1984) gave students a solved prototype task and analogous tasks. Some were also given a conceptual model with the solved prototype, whilst others were given a general procedure for applying the prototype model to the transfer items. The procedure helped considerably for the transfer items which were least like the prototype item. His definition of transfer echoes that given here, by seeing two elements 'the generation and/or application of a rule for solving a set of problems'.

This suggests that attention must be given to *how* students attempt to transfer the content of their learning, and that this is especially helpful when the content items are very different. This confirms Gray's (1985) view that the focus on process is functional when the contexts between which transfer is attempted are very different.

In the interviews in Case Illustration I both student and teacher showed this meta-learning ability by reflecting on the processes utilized during the placement. One response to the problem of how to help students learn more effectively is to reject the study-skills approach (Gibbs 1977 and 1981) and focus instead on meta-learning skills. Biggs (1985) quotes Wagner and Sternberg (1984) in support:

> Emphasis on metacognitive training does result in some degree of durability and transfer.

Wollman (1984) also points in the same direction:

> Minimal instruction enabled most students to acquire not only effective concepts for organising and transferring knowledge in a problem domain, but also a first introduction to the higher order concepts of organisation and transfer.

Maier (1984) similarly distinguishes first-order, incremental change and second-order, transformational changes in learning which can reframe a student's experience. His first-order 'concrete, step-by-step learning' is a reproductive, serialist conception. His second-order 'involves a paradigm shift so impactful that students can transfer their learning to corresponding situations . . .' This transfer is of the content of learning, not the process. A further paradigmatic shift, to a third-order, would encompass being able to transform learning processes through learning to learn (though Maier does not recognize a third such order).

Indeed, more recent work might confirm some of this. Boreham (1985) reports improved transfer by 'lowering fidelity of simulation' so that an intervening process of generalization is required to transfer learning. The need to be able to generalize before transfer can take place is reinforced in other ways, too. Kolb (1976) emphasizes a four stage cycle of concrete experience, reflection, the formation of abstract concepts and generalizations, and hypotheses to be tested in future action – which led to new experiences which in turn generate further relection, and so on. The notion of conceptual pyramids, which Badger (1985a) and Harris (1983) found helpful, in which higher orders subsume lower orders, can help the recognition of different orders of generality and specificity (CCETSW, 1979). Russell's Theory of Logical Types (1910) helps to distinguish a class from its members; and to recognize that some higher order classes are not merely more general, but they frame and give meaning to the classes below. This might be a fruitful direction for further work in helping to develop third-order (Stage Three) conceptions.

Keane (1987) covers similar ground in relation to a cognitive theory of analogy, where he emphasises the importance of functionally related attributes and higher order relations if analogies are to be of use. This is a special case of transferring learning – here from the analogy to the target domain (via generalizations and higher order concepts), but which also requires the intervening generalizing and reapplication process.

This allows a critical reflection on earlier work on transfer. Bruner (1960) says: 'a general idea . . . can be used as a basis for recognizing subsequent problems as special cases of the ideas originally mastered', but like Ausubel (1968) his focus is on the content of the transfer rather than the learning process.

Much of the literature on transfer is similarly content-focused. For example Royer and Cable (1976) asked five groups of students to read pairs of passages to show transfer was more likely where pre-existing 'knowledge bridges' existed from conceptual frameworks in the first of the passages. It is possible to reconsider their findings in the light of the model developed in this study. The transfer tasks are content-related surface learning tasks, and the two passages which are less 'relevant' and do not promote transfer seem, on the basis of the material given, to be broadly focused, meaning-oriented pieces. If this is so, it may be that subjects were oriented to expecting the second passage and the subsequent questions to be of this kind (i.e. deep learning). The Royer and Cable findings may represent a mis-match of Stage Two expectations of learning induced by the passage, and a more simplistic Stage One test of whether transfer (of content) had taken place.

Eysenck and Warren Piper (1987) emphasize how the conditions under which learning is tested may influence results, and cite Nitsch (1977) to show that the transfer of learning to new and different contexts was more successful in identifying concepts than in same-context groups. This ability to discriminate generalizations from examples, and vice-versa is central to the definition of the transfer of learning described here. Laurillard (1987) discusses these issues in the light of Marton and Saljo's work:

> One common difficulty has been identified by Ference Marton and Roger Saljo. This is the inability to perceive the 'figure-ground' structure in a text. Many academic texts have this form, where the figure-ground refers to the principle-example, the main argument-evidence, the generalisation-instance . . . replicated studies . . . show that within any group, some students will report the text as being about the principle . . . others report the same text as being about the content of the example (Marton and Wenestam 1979).

Laurillard goes on to relate these differences to those between deep and surface learning, but they also contribute to the steps identified in the learning process required to transfer learning – unless students (and teachers) can sort out levels of generality and specificity, they will not be able to accomplish transfer through an intervening generalization. Badger (1985a) says:

> I do not find it easy to envisage what Gardiner had in mind when he wrote about some students needing extra help 'to make the necessary distinctions

between levels of generality and specificity of concepts in order that they can transfer their learning from one area of practice to another. (Gardiner 1984b)'

It seems that some tutors and supervisors may need such help as well. Not only are these key elements in helping students to become versatile and effective learners, but they are also an area where staff development work needs to be concentrated.

8

Implications for the Future of Social Work Education: and Further Developments of this Research

8.1 Some implications of the study for social work education

CCETSW has been reviewing its policies for qualifying training in social work for much of the past decade. The debates about improving social work education have given considerable attention to the resourcing, structure, patterns, content and outcomes of courses. The length of training was seen as the key element in improving standards, with courses being extended to a minimum of three years. In the absence of funds to increase the *quantity* of training, social work educators need to look at how to improve the *quality* of the courses, regardless of their length. These issues have been substantially addressed elsewhere (Gardiner 1988).

Planning for a new unified social work award gave attention to the increased *amount* which social workers have to learn, especially in relation to relevant legislation. This may run the risk, however, of inducing more surface-reproductive patterns of teaching, learning and assessment by reinforcing a focus on the *content* of learning at the expense of the *learning process*. Competent professional practice, in social work as elsewhere, will depend not only on students' memory of what they were taught during training, but also on their abilities to learn from experience and make consequent professional judgements. Therefore it is necessary to ensure that teaching approaches, curriculum design, assessment forms and methods, internal monitoring and evaluation schemes and external validation strategies are all capable of promoting deep constructive approaches to learning, and versatility in teaching and learning approaches.

Newble and Entwistle (1986) may have been describing some parts of social work education when they say of medical education:

> We believe that a high proportion of medical schools have assessment schemes which fail to evaluate many of the most important curriculum objectives. All too often, examinations evaluate little more than the recall of

factual knowledge. Where this is so, the habit of students who use a surface approach is likely to be reinforced, strategic learners will tend to adopt a surface approach and even students who prefer a deep approach may be forced to rote learn if the amount to be remembered is too great.

The implications of this research for the enterprise of social work education as a whole are unambiguous: the nature and quality of student learning is the key indicator of improving standards in the courses, so attention must be directed to identifying and promoting the kinds of approaches to learning which students will need if they are to achieve the required learning outcomes for competent professional practice.

It is possible to begin to identify the key elements in a strategy to improve the *quality* of student learning. At the heart of the present research, and other related research, are the conceptions which teachers and students have of the activity of *learning* itself. If they are found to be at Stage One in the model developed in this study, then urgent attention needs to be given to transforming those conceptions. Marton and Saljo (1976b) confirm that:

> . . . students may need to refocus their attention on the underlying meaning of what they are required to study and that this process could be helped by ensuring that the assessment procedures demand deep-level processing.

The research findings here and elsewhere point to the key role of assessment in determining the nature and quality of teaching and learning. It should be noted that this does not mean the *form* of the assessment (essays, exams, project work etc.); instead, it does mean *what kinds of learning* are required and valued. It is important to remember that Dearden (1976) showed, despite many changes in laboratory teaching, it was eventually a small change in the way laboratory notebooks were assessed that brought about the desired changes in students' learning approaches.

Assessment, though, is only one element of the context of learning and the approach of the teacher is also an important determinant of the student's approach (Laurillard 1978; Gibbs, Morgan and Taylor 1982 and 1984). This study has presented evidence demonstrating the impact of supervisors' approaches to teaching on students' approaches to learning. However, simplistic matching of teaching and learning approaches is not enough, because although students may well have 'relatively consistent preferences . . . to learn in characteristic ways – their learning styles,' it is vital to look at 'the actual approaches to learning which they adopt in a particular context' (Newble and Entwistle 1986).

Biggs (1985) suggests that we should look at two broad options for teachers (and validators?):

1. To accept the student's orientation as given, and match instructional objectives, teaching processes, and evaluation procedures . . . to maximize *content* learning;
2. To attempt to change the student's orientation where it is seen to be maladaptive in order to maximize *process* learning.

The findings reported in this book, however, show that attempts to improve the quality of teaching and learning in social work education will need to include evaluating the stage that both teachers and learners have reached in their conception of the learning in which they are engaged. Staff development programmes for teachers (for tutors as well as supervisors) will be important in this process. Whilst this research was being written up, a qualitative study of the tutorial system in social work education was published (Bamford 1987) which gathered data from tutors, students, supervisors and past students to explore the role of the tutor. His work does not refer to any of the research in adult learning reviewed in this study, and his work is constrained by some of the assumptions and concepts of the classical model (which is thereby shown to permeate thinking about tutorials as well as supervision). Two areas of Bamford's work are of particular interest. One is his finding about matching students and supervisors 'so that predictable clashes on personality or ideological grounds are avoided'. The other is about the credibility of the tutors in terms of closeness to current practice. Marton (1981), has shown that a 'phenomenographic' second-order perspective would be needed to elicit conceptions of the role of tutors. Bamford's data would be susceptible to re-analysis using the model developed here, and it would be useful for some developments of this kind to take place.

Although individual teacher-learner interactions have been concentrated upon, there are wider implications of the work in relation to curriculum design, and the structure of training systems. Particular attention should be given to the impact of college- and agency-based approaches to teaching on how students perceive what is required of them. Innovative course structures, and progressive approaches to teaching and learning, are unlikely to produce deep outcomes and to develop professional competence, if students perceive that what is valued (particularly through their perceptions of assessment requirements) is only surface-reproductive learning.

This is the central question facing course providers and the validating body in improving qualifying training: how to ensure a high national minimum standard, by specifying required student competencies, without making such outcomes difficult, or even impossible, to achieve because the forms of assessment induce surface-reproductive learning. There is also some limited evidence that when validating bodies make too many requirements of courses, or put too much detail into the required content of student assessment, courses may respond (just as students might) in surface-reproductive ways to meet those requirements.

At present, there is no systematic examination of the impact of assessment on the quality of student learning in social work courses. Until and unless such studies are undertaken, attempts to improve the standard of qualifying training by specifying student competencies at outcome will be impossible to evaluate, and claims that longer training will improve standards (CCETSW 1987) will be difficult to justify. Such evaluations could focus on the kinds of teaching and assessment which might promote (or at least, not constrain) higher level interactions. Biggs (1985) quotes Brown (1984) about this:

. . . some form of metacognitive theory could offer valuable contributions to the arguments about a core curriculum. Selection of problem-solving tasks . . . might then be based not only upon subjects deemed to be valuable in terms of their contents, but also on essential metacognitive skills . . . Metacognition may succeed where formal disciplines failed.

In parallel, there is a need to monitor standards not just in individual teaching and learning interactions, but also in courses as a whole (Adelman and Alexander 1983; Gardiner 1987b; Moodie 1986). Increased attention currently being given to self-monitoring and self-evaluation, together with the introduction of teacher-appraisal in higher education, emphasize the importance of developing qualitative methodologies to identify and foster quality in student learning.

8.2   Further developments of the approach and model from this research study

Although some implications for social work education have been identified, this study is only a beginning contribution. Further evaluative research is necessary to replicate and extend these findings and the preliminary account of the model. College-based parts of social work courses should be susceptible to the same kinds of evaluation; and social work training could be evaluated alongside developments in other professional and vocational preparation. This kind of research would provide a rational basis for policy development in future, and could generate materials for staff development programmes. There are, in addition, implications for the supervision of social work staff in agencies, especially in relation to their own continuing professional development.

I have, in the past year or so, begun to gather qualitative data on the conceptions which social work tutors, supervisors and students have of learning, teaching and education generally; and of the relationship between theory and practice, the purpose of practice placements, and the purpose of supervision. This follow up study (which has so far included more than 250 respondents) has produced some striking findings, which are only sketched here. About half of all the teacher respondents have given Stage One conceptions in answer to the general questions: 'What do you mean by learning?' 'What do you mean by teaching?' 'What do you mean by education?' This is a worrying finding if it accurately reflects how they conceive of these notions in qualifying courses. But it becomes more worrying when the answers to the specific questions are also taken into account: around half of those who had Stage Two or Stage Three conceptions of the general educational concepts gave Stage One responses to the questions about the relation of theory to practice, and to the purposes of placements and supervision.

If indeed about threequarters of all those teaching on social work courses (in colleges and agencies) have conceptions which seem likely to constrain teacher-learner interactions in placements to Level One patterns, then the case for a major staff development programme to help them change the level of those conceptions is very strong.

A second follow up area of the research is a study which is looking at components of training courses, and courses as a whole, and relating these to students' and teachers' conceptions of learning. Some tutors who are involved in this project have expressed concern that the experience of being a student on their courses may be of predominantly Level One interactions – even for those students who joined the course with higher order conceptions of learning. It would be immensely valuable to begin to tease out precisely what constrains students to acting in surface-reproductive ways in those courses. Both of these follow up studies will be reported in due course.

The study has also prompted similar work on supervision of qualified staff within agencies, and in other professional training programmes (including engineering, where students' conceptions of learning are being analysed in relation to examination performance, and to individual qualitative assessments by an external examiner to the course).

A rather different set of recent developments has emerged from utilizing the model more widely than in teacher-learner interactions. A joint paper, which brought together research findings from this study with recent developments in training and organizational development (Gardiner and Mathias 1988) demonstrated the very close connection between conceptions of 'learning', of 'training' and of 'organization'. Thus, the three stage model, based on three characteristic patterns of interaction, was found to explain experiences of training and staff development in much broader areas. In essence, the model was found to be useful in explaining interactions between individuals; between individuals and a group; and between groups; in their various consultations and negotiations around training initiatives and staff development programmes. Recurrent problems like poor take up of courses, lack of application and commitment, hostility from other departments or organizations, were found to be associated with mis-matched levels of conception about change enterprises (including education and training).

8.3   Summary and conclusions

This study used the author's own experience to highlight shortcomings in the explanations derived from the classical model of casework supervision. Despite the fact that practice placements take up to half of the time in training, teaching and learning in supervision is under-researched.

The literature published in the United Kingdom was reviewed, and found to be heavily reliant upon earlier American social casework supervision literature. The key feature was the 'leakage' of concepts from the therapeutic arena to describing the supervisory process, which led to continuing debate about whether supervision was therapy. The form of teaching associated with that model is traditional, hierarchical, and directed towards students learning the 'right' way to practise.

Students who did not learn in the expected ways were pathologized or called 'uneducable'. New supervisors were placed in hierarchical relationships with college tutors. Later contributions to this literature, and the autobiographical accounts, show the persistence of the language and assumptions.

The research problem was to produce descriptive data which could contribute to formulating other interpretations of teaching and learning in supervision, and which could lead to the development of conceptual models and frameworks arising from the findings and grounded in them.

The literature on methodological approaches to educational research was surveyed, and the advantages of qualitative methods of collecting and presenting data to address this research problem were described. The design of the first stage of data collection reflected these qualitative perspectives with a broad view of how supervisors construed teaching and learning (using a questionnaire), and a narrow focused case study of supervision through an entire placement (by tape-recording those sessions).

These findings highlighted the importance of styles or approaches to learning, and the stage of conception of learning reached by supervisors and students. The research literature on adult learning in those areas was reviewed, and much that was of potential value was found in studies published by that time in Sweden, England, and the United States. The Swedish work showed the very close relation between qualitative differences in approaches to differences in the outcomes of learning; and the impact on these approaches of the conceptions students had of 'learning'. Some of the work in England identified different learning strategies, and looked also at the effect of match and mismatch of learning and teaching styles. Other English work showed the extent to which these differences in approach were dependent on students' perceptions of the learning task, and the context in which the learning took place. American work showed developmental stages through which adult learners pass – from a polarized conception of absolutes, with rights and wrongs known to authorities, to recognizing that knowledge is contextual and relative, and that personal values and commitment to them determine how adults relate to knowledge and authorities.

In the light of this review, the major stage of data collection was designed, using interview methods allowing follow up of some material gathered in the first stage, and to include other supervisors. Data were collected on learning styles alongside the interview material, and feedback discussions which checked the accuracy of descriptions and interpretations were included in the study. In some of the cases, additional data were gathered where this seemed appropriate. Thus a tutor was interviewed in relation to one placement, and tapes of supervision sessions were gathered in relation to others.

The findings of this stage were presented as case illustrations selected for their contribution to model building. Elements of the model were emphasized within each case illustration and then brought together in the development of a schematic framework which accounted for the teaching and learning interactions seen in supervision. This model is founded on the conceptions which teachers and learners have of learning, and the impact of these conceptions in constraining possible levels of interaction in supervision.

Three qualitatively different levels of interaction were identified. Level One was associated with a surface-reproductive conception of learning; Level Two was associated with a deep-constructive conception of learning, and a search for meaning through the learner's involvement in the learning. The difference between Levels One and Two was a focus on process of learning (Level Two) rather than a focus on the content of learning (Level One). Level Three interactions were characterized by meta-learning – reflection on various approaches to learning, and choosing from a repertoire of approaches to meet the requirements of a task, so that learning to learn enhanced the process of the transfer of learning.

A three stage model of these interactions was devised in which each higher order conception of learning subsumed the one below. Problems of mis-matched levels of conception were more acute when one or other participant (especially the supervisor) had only a Stage One conception of learning, which constrained supervision to Level One interactions.

The findings and the model were considered in the light of more recent research into student learning. Considerable congruence between the findings of this study and developments elsewhere was found. The present study, looking specifically at teaching and learning interactions in professional training is illuminative, and a number of areas for further research were identified. Some of these projects are now underway.

8.4   Final thoughts

This book began by saying it was about quality – quality in education, and quality in evaluation methodology. To gather data to illumine and explain interactions in supervision necessitated the development of methodologies that were the equivalent of Stage Three in the model, if they were to capture Level Three-type interactions. Such methods validate, even demand, the involvement of a researcher in the field of study and the process of data gathering, when interpretations and meanings are also the target of the study. The methodology can be characterized in three levels, in parallel with the interactive model of teaching and learning:

1. At the first level is the need to record, describe and report qualitative data – and one's own experience is a valuable place to start.
2. At the second level, the meanings ascribed to such experiences need to be gathered, and the data from the previous level need to be re-examined, so that patterns and generalizations can be deduced.
3. At the third level, those meanings, patterns and generalizations need to be systematized into an explanatory scheme or model, and re-evaluated in the light of further data collection (which may include literature searches as well as primary data).

This reflective, recursive process is the basis of grounded theory. The focus and methodology of this evaluation has provided an initial formulation of a model. Further evaluative studies, from the perspective of how people construe their world, utilizing qualitative methods like those developed in this study, could provide the basis of a *new paradigm of learning* in professional and vocational education and training (Gardiner 1986b).

However, the study is not intended as an alternative 'right' answer to the casework supervision model. Perry (1981) recognized that an analogous process to the developmental scheme he devised for college students' intellectual development may be taking place in the conceptual developments and model-building of researchers into student learning. If that is so, then there is a need to produce a number of alternatives (within different paradigms) to the single Right Answer in the classical supervision model. Social work education might then reach at least the equivalent of contextual, relativistic reasoning (Position Five) in Perry's scheme; or at least the recognition of diversity (Stage Two) in the model presented here.

This book, and the research study it reports, can be considered as a case study in how to undertake a piece of qualitative research. This qualitative methodology is congruent with the model of learning, and the account of the learning process, developed in the study, because through reflection it establishes salience, patterns, and generalizations which are then evaluated for their usefulness in new and different situations. It is offered here to help reassure others in professional and vocational education that it is possible, and desirable, to undertake qualitative evaluations of the nature and quality of student learning. These are not only legitimate methods of evaluation, but are essential if we are to improve the quality and effectiveness of teaching and learning for professional competence.

Chambers' Dictionary defines *Anatomy* as 'the art of dissecting any organized body: the science of the structure of the body learned by dissection'. It is to be hoped that studies like *The Anatomy of Supervision* contribute to the art of qualitative evaluation in dissecting teaching and learning processes; and to the science of model- and theory-building of the structure of education for professional competence.

Bibliography

Adcock, M., Craig, D., Gardiner, D. and Jaques, D. (1977). Much binding on Plumstead Marshes. *Health and Social Services Journal*, August.

Adelman, C. and Alexander, R. (1983). *The Self-Evaluating Institution: Principles and Practice in the Management of Educational Change*. London, Methuen.

Austin, L. (1952). Basic principles of supervision. *Social Casework*, December.

Ausubel, D. (1968). *Educational Psychology: A Cognitive View*. New York, Holt, Rinehart and Winston.

Badger, D. (1985a). Learning for transfer: a further contribution. *Issues in Social Work Education*, 5(1), 63–6.

Badger, D. (1985b). Building bridges: The transfer of learning between field and residential work, in Harris, R. *et al.* (eds) *Educating Social Workers*. Leicester, ATSWE.

Bamford, D. (1987). *The Personal Tutor in Social Work Education*. Bedford, Cranfield Press.

Bateson, G., Jackson, D., Haley, J. and Weakland, J. (1956). Towards a theory of schizophrenia. *Behavioural Science*, 1(4).

Biggs, J. (1978). Individual and group differences in study processes. *British Journal of Educational Psychology*, 48, 266–79.

Biggs, J. (1985). The role of metalearning in study processes. *British Journal of Educational Psychology*, 55, 185–212.

Boreham, N. (1985). Transfer of training in the generation of diagnostic hypotheses. *British Journal of Educational Psychology*, 55, 213–23.

Brandon, J. and Davies, M. (1979). The limits of competence in social work: the assessment of marginal students in social work education. *British Journal of Social Work*, 9(3), 295–347.

Brown, G. (1984). Metacognition: new insights into old problems? *British Journal of Educational Studies*, 32, 213–19.

Bruner, J. (1960). *The Process of Education*. Cambridge, Harvard University Press.

Burnham, J. and Harris, Q. (1985). Therapy, supervision, consultation: different levels of a system, in Campbell, D. and Draper, R. (eds) *Applications of Systemic Family Therapy*. London, Academic Press.

Carroll, L. (1877). *Through the Looking Glass*. London, Macmillan.

Casson, P. (1982). *Social Work Courses: Their Structure and Content*. Study 5, London, CCETSW.

Curnock, K. (1975). *Student Units in Social Work Education*. Paper 11, London, CCETSW.

CCETSW (1977). *Consultative Document 3 – An Analysis of Responses and Some Policy Implications* by Gardiner, D. London, CCETSW.

CCETSW (1979). *Training for Work with Mentally Handicapped People*. London, CCETSW.
CCETSW (1981). *Guidelines for Courses Leading to the CQSW* (revised 1981) London, CCETSW.
CCETSW (1983). *Research into Practice Teaching*. Study 6, London, CCETSW.
CCETSW (1984). *Implementing the New Requirements for CQSW Courses. An Analysis of the Plans of Educational Institutions*. Paper 15.2, London, CCETSW.
CCETSW (1987). *Care for Tomorrow. The Case for Reform of Education and Training for Social Workers and other Care Staff*, London, CCETSW.
Dahlgren, L. and Marton, F. (1978). Students' conceptions of learning matter: an aspect of learning and teaching in higher education. *Studies in Higher Education*, 3(1).
Danbury, H. (1979). (Second Edition, 1986). *Teaching Practical Social Work*, Aldershot. Gower.
Dearden, G. (1976). *Assessment in an Electrical and Electronic Engineering Laboratory: A Case Study*. Conference on the Teaching of Electronic Engineering Courses, Hull, in Elton and Laurillard, *op. cit.* (1979).
Deed, D. (1962). Danger of stereotypes in student supervision. *Case Conference*, 9(1).
Dinerman, M. (1983). Educating social workers: British patterns from an American perspective. *International Social Work*, XXVI, (2), 27–32.
Ebbinghaus, H. (1885). *Uber das Gedachtnis*. Leipzig, Dincker and Humboldt, in Saljo, *op. cit.* (1987).
Elton, L. and Laurillard, D. (1979). Trends in research on student learning. *Studies in Higher Education*, 4(1), 87–102.
Entwistle, N. (1977). Strategies of learning and studying: recent research findings. *British Journal of Educational Studies*, XXV(3), 225–38.
Entwistle, N. (1978). Learning processes and strategies IV – knowledge structures and styles of learning: a summary of Pask's recent research. *British Journal of Educational Psychology*, 48, 255–65.
Entwistle, N. (1984). *Contrasting Perspectives on Learning*, in Marton, F., Hounsell, D. and Entwistle, N. (eds) *op. cit.* (1984).
Entwistle, N. (1987). A model of the teaching-learning process, in Richardson, J., Eysenck, M. and Warren Piper, D. (eds) *op. cit.* (1987).
Entwistle, N. and Hanley, M. (1977). Personality, cognitive style and students' learning strategies. *Higher Education Bulletin*, 6(1), 23–43.
Entwistle, N. and Ramsden, P. (1983). *Understanding Student Learning*. London, Croom Helm.
Evans, D. (1987). The centrality of practice in social work education. *Issues in Social Work Education*, 7(2).
Eysenck, H. (1965). *Fact and Fiction in Psychology*. London, Penguin.
Eysenck, M. and Warren Piper, D. (1987). A word is worth a thousand pictures, in Richardson, J., Eysenck, M. and Warren Piper, D. (eds) *op. cit.* (1987).
Flavell, J. (1976). Metacognitive aspects of problem solving, in Resnick, L. (ed.) *The Nature of Intelligence*. New Jersey, Laurence Erlbaum.
Freire, P. (1972). *Pedagogy of the Oppressed*. London, Sheed and Wards.
Gardiner, D. (1972). *Mental Illness: Myth, Metaphor or Madness*. Southampton, Wessex Regional School of Psychiatry.
Gardiner, D. (1984a). Social work education and the transfer of learning – a comment. *Issues in Social Work Education*, 4(1), 55–7.
Gardiner, D. (1984b). Learning for transfer. *Issues in Social Work Education*, 4(2), 95–105.
Gardiner, D. (1984c). Evaluation of educational innovation. Feedback to evaluators. *Evaluation Newsletter*, 8(1), 4–10.

Gardiner, D. (1985). *Ethnic Minorities and Social Work Training*. Paper 21.1. London, CCETSW.

Gardiner, D. (1986a). *Learning for Transfer*. Plenary Paper 678/86. Conference on Staff Development and Supervision for the Human Services. Dubrovnik, Yugoslavia, Inter-University Centre of Post-Graduate Studies.

Gardiner, D. (1986b). *Towards a Paradigm of Learning in Social Work Education*. Plenary Paper 679/86. Conference on Staff Development and Supervision for the Human Services. Dubrovnik, Yugoslavia, Inter-University Centre of Post-Graduate Studies.

Gardiner, D. (1987a). Generic and specialist issues in social work education. *Issues in Social Work Education*, 7(1), 47–52.

Gardiner, D. (1987b). Towards internal monitoring and evaluation of social work courses. *Issues in Social Work Education*, 7(1), 53–5.

Gardiner, D. (1987c). *Teaching and Learning in Social Work Practice Placements: A Study of Process in Professional Training*. Ph.D. Thesis, London, University of London Institute of Education.

Gardiner, D. (1988). Improving students' learning – setting an agenda for quality in the 1990s. *Issues in Social Work Education*, 8(1).

Gardiner, D. and Gray, J. (1989). How to judge the quality of learning systems: some case examples in the evaluation of professional education and staff development programmes. Educational Technology Informational Conference, 1989.

Gardiner, D. and Mathias, P. (1988). *Improving Learning – The Impact of Conceptions of Learning on Professional Training and Staff Development Programmes*. Educational Technology International Conference, 1988; and Kogan Page, *Aspects of Educational Technology*, Procedings of ETIC, 1988.

Gardiner/CCETSW (1978). *The Development of Practice Teaching and Practice Placements on CQSW Courses*. Professional Studies and Qualifications Committee, Paper 78/56, London, CCETSW.

Garrett, A. (1954). Learning through supervision. *Boston, Smith College Studies in Social Work*, XXIV(2).

Gibbs, G. (1977). Can students be taught how to study? *Higher Education Bulletin*, 5(2), 107–18.

Gibbs, G. (1981). *Teaching Students to Learn*. Milton Keynes, Open University Press.

Gibbs, G., Morgan, A. and Taylor, E. (1982). Why students don't learn. *Institutional Research Review*, 1, 9–32.

Gibbs, G., Morgan, A. and Taylor, E. (1984). The world of the learner, in Marton, F., Hounsell, D. and Entwistle, N. (eds) *op. cit.* (1984).

Glaser, B. and Strauss, A. (1967). *The Discovery of Grounded Theory*. New York, Aldine.

Goodman, N. (1978). *Ways of Worldmaking*. Hassocks, Sussex, The Harvester Press.

Gorer, G. (1966). Psychoanalysis in the world, in Rycroft, C. (ed.) *op. cit.* (1966).

Gray, J. (1985). Learning for transfer – the special case of practising social work in different countries. *Issues in Social Work Education*, 5(2), 145–9.

Gray, J. (1986). Family Therapy Training: Teaching and Learning for Clinical Practice. Unpublished Dissertation. London, Institute for Family Therapy.

Hadley, R. (1984). *Decentralising Social Services: A Model for Change*. London, Bedford Square Press.

Hamilton, D., Jenkins, D., King, C., MacDonald, B. and Parlett, M. (eds) (1977). *Beyond the Numbers Game*. Basingstoke, Macmillan Education.

Hardiker, P. and Barker, M. (1981). *Theories of Practice in Social Work*. London, Academic Press.

Harris, R. (1983). Social work education and the transfer of learning. *Issues in Social Work Education*, 3(2), 103–17.

Heywood, J. (1964). *An Introduction to Teaching Casework Skills*. London, Routledge and Kegan Paul.

Holloway, C. (1977). *Learning and Instruction*. Open University Course D303, Block 4, Units 22–23, Milton Keynes, Open University Press.

Howarth, E. (1961). An introduction to casework supervision. *Case Conference*, 8(6).

Hudson, J. (1984). A new paradigm for social work. *Social Work Education* 4(1), 2–6.

Hudson, L. (1966). *Contrary Imaginations*. London, Methuen.

Illich, I. (1970). *Deschooling Society*. Harmondsworth, Penguin.

Illich, I. (1977). Disabling professions, in Illich, I. *et al.* (eds) *Disabling Professions*. London, Marion Boyars.

Jaques, D. (1982). Tug-of-war in Thamesmead: evaluating a community-based project. *Evaluation Newsletter*, 6(1).

Keane, M. (1987). Cognitive theory of analogy, in Richardson *et al.* (eds) *op. cit.* (1987).

Kent, B. (1969). *Social Work Supervision in Practice*. Oxford, Pergamon Press.

Kings Fund. (1986). *Thamesmead Interdisciplinary Project*. London, Kings Fund.

Knowles, M. (1972). Innovations in teaching styles and approaches based on adult learning. *Journal of Education for Social Work*, 8(2), 32–9.

Knowles, M. (1978). *The Adult Learner – A Neglected Species*. (Second Edition). Houston, Gulf Publishing.

Kolb, D. (1976). *Learning Styles Inventory Technical Manual*. Boston, McBer.

Kuhn, T. (1970). *The Structure of Scientific Revolutions*. Chicago, University of Chicago Press.

Laurillard, D. (1978). *A Study of the Relationship Between Some of the Cognitive and Contextual Factors in Student Learning*. Ph.D. Thesis. Guildford, University of Surrey.

Laurillard, D. (1987). *The different forms of learning in psychology and education*, in Richardson, J., Eysenck, M. and Warren Piper, D. (eds) *op. cit.* (1987).

Lawton, D. (1980). *The politics of curriculum evaluation*, in *Issues in Methodology*. Milton Keynes, Open University Curriculum in Action Course Materials.

Liddle, H. and Saba, G. (1983). On context replication: the isomorphic relation of training and therapy. *Journal of Strategic and Systemic Therapies*, 2(2), 3–11.

MacDonald, B. (1976). Evaluation and the control of education, in Tawney, D. (ed.) *Curriculum Evaluation Today*. Basingstoke, Macmillan Education.

MacDonald, B. and Walker, R. (1977). *Case-study and the philosophy of educational research*, in Hamilton, D. *et al.* (eds) *op. cit.* (1977).

Maier, H. (1984). A simple but powerful concept poses a challenge for the teaching and learning of social work practice. *Social Work Education*, 4(1).

Mann, S. (1987). On knowing ourselves as learners and researchers, in Richardson, J., Eysenck, M. and Warren Piper D. (eds) *op. cit.* (1987).

Marton, F. (1975). What does it take to learn, in Entwistle, N. and Hounsell, D. (eds) *How Students Learn*. Lancaster, Centre for Post-Compulsory Education.

Marton, F. (1981). Phenomenography – describing conceptions of the world around us. *Instructional Science*, 10, 177–200.

Marton, F., Hounsell, D. and Entwistle, N. (eds) (1984). *The Experience of Learning*. Edinburgh, Scottish Academic Press.

Marton, F and Saljo, R. (1976a). On qualitative differences in learning: I – Outcome and process. *British Journal of Educational Psychology*, 46, 4–11.

Marton, F. and Saljo, R. (1976b). On qualitative differences in learning: II – Outcome as a function of the learner's conception of the task. *British Journal of Educational Psychology*, 46, 115–27.

Marton, F. and Wenestam, C-G. (1979). Qualitative differences in understanding and retention of the main point in some texts based on the principle-example structure, in Gruneberg, P. *et al.* (eds) *Practical Aspects of Memory*, Academic Press.

Michael, G. (1976). Content and Method in Fieldwork Teaching. Unpublished Ph.D. Thesis, University of Edinburgh.

Miller, C. (1983). Evaluation Research Methods – a Guide, in *Research in Practice Teaching*, Study 6, London, CCETSW.

Miller, C. and Parlett, M. (1973). *Up to the Mark*. Occasional Paper 13, Centre for Research in Educational Sciences, University of Edinburgh.

Minuchin, S. (1974). *Families and Family Therapy*. London, Tavistock Publications.

Moodie, G. (ed.) (1986). *Standards and Criteria in Higher Education*. Guildford, SRHE and NFER-Nelson.

Morrell, E. (1979). The Assessment of Fieldwork Placements. Unpublished M. Phil. Thesis, University of Leicester.

Newble, D. and Entwistle, N. (1986). Learning styles and approaches: implications for medical education. *Medical Education*, 20, 162–75.

Nitsch, K. (1977). Structuring Decontextualized Forms of Knowledge. Unpublished Ph.D. Thesis, Vanderbilt University, Nashville, Tennessee; in Eysenck, M. and Warren Piper, D. *op. cit.* (1987).

Orwell, G. (1945). *Nineteen Eighty-Four,* London, Secker and Warburg.

Parlett, M. (1970). The syllabus-bound student, in Hudson, L. (ed.) *The Ecology of Human Intelligence*. Harmondsworth, Penguin.

Parlett, M. and Hamilton, D. (1971). *Evaluation as Illumination: a new approach to the study of innovatory programmes*. Occasional Paper 9, Centre for Research in Educational Sciences, University of Edinburgh.

Parsloe, P. (1982). The learning process, *Community Care*, 429, 16 September.

Pask, G. (1976a). Conversational techniques in the study and practice of education. *British Journal of Educational Psychology*, 46, 12–25.

Pask, G. (1976b) Styles and strategies of learning. *British Journal of Educational Psychology*, 46, 128–48.

Pask, G. and Scott, B. (1972). Learning strategies and individual competence. *International Journal of Man-Machine Studies*, 4, 217–53.

Pask, G. and Scott, B. (1973). CASTE: A System for Exhibiting Learning Strategies and Regulating Uncertainties. *International Journal of Man-Machine Studies*, 5, 17–52.

Patton, M. (1978). *Utilisation-Focussed Evaluation*. London, Sage.

Patton, M. (1980). *Qualitative Evaluation Methods*. London, Sage.

Perry, W. (1970). *Forms of Intellectual and Ethical Development in the College Years: a Scheme*. New York, Holt, Rinehart and Winston.

Perry, W. (1981). Cognitive and ethical growth: the making of meaning, in Chickering *et al. The Modern American College*. San Francisco, Jossey-Bass.

Pettes, D. (1967 and 1979: Second Edition). *Staff and Student Supervision*. London, George Allen and Unwin.

Pincus, A. and Minahan, A. (1973). *Social Work Practice: Model and Method*. Illinois, Peacock.

Pratte, R. (1981). Metaphorical models and curriculum theory. *Curriculum Inquiry*, 11(4).

Ramsden, P. (1979). Student learning and perceptions of the academic environment. *Higher Education*, 8, 411–27.

Richardson, J. (1987). Research in Education and Cognitive Psychology, in Richardson, J., Eysenck, M. and Warren Piper, D. (eds) *op. cit.* (1987).

Richardson, J., Eysenck, M. and Warren Piper, D. (eds) (1987). *Student Learning*, Milton Keynes, SRHE and Open University Press.

Rogers, C. (1961). *On Becoming a Person: a Therapist's View of Psychotherapy*. London, Constable.

Rogers, C. (1969). *Freedom to Learn*. Columbus, Ohio, Charles Merritt.

Royer, J. and Cable, G. (1976). Illustrations, analogies, and facilitative transfer in prose learning. *Journal of Educational Psychology*, 68, 205–9.

Russell, B. (1910). *Principia Mathematica* (with Whitehead, A.) Cambridge, Cambridge University Press.

Ryan, D. (1987) The impermeable membrane, in Richardson, J., Eysenck, M. and Warren Piper, D. (eds) *op. cit.* (1987).

Rycroft, C. (ed.) (1966). *Psychoanalysis Observed*. Harmondsworth, Penguin.

Saljo, R. (1975). *Qualitative Differences in Learning as a Function of the Learner's Conception of the Task*. Studies in Educational Sciences 14, University of Göteborg.

Saljo, R. (1979). *Learning in the Learner's Perspective I – Some Commonsense Conceptions*. Reports from the Institute of Education No. 77, University of Göteborg.

Saljo, R. (1987). The Educational Construction of Learning, in Richardson, J., Eysenck, M. and Warren Piper, D. (eds) *op. cit.*

Sawdon, D. (1986). *Making Connections in Practice Teaching*. London, NISW.

Shaw, I and Walton, R. (1978). Education for practice: former students' attitudes to a social work course. *Contemporary Social Work Education*, 2(1), 15–29.

Sheldon, B. (1986). Social work effectiveness experiments: Review and implications. *British Journal of Social Work*, 16(2), 223–42.

Smith, M. (1977). *The Underground and Education*. London, Methuen.

Stake, R. (1977). Responsive Evaluation, in Hamilton, D. *et al.* (eds) *Beyond the Numbers Game*. Basingstoke, Macmillan Education.

Suboda, N. (1986). *Supervision in the Human Services*. Plenary Paper 680/86. Conference on Staff Development in the Human Services. Dubrovnik, Yugoslavia, Inter-University Centre of Postgraduate Studies.

Svensson, L. (1976). *Study Skill and Learning*. Acta Universitatis Gothoburgensis.

Syson, L. with Baginsky, M. (1981). *Learning to Practise – A Study of Practice Placements in Courses Leading to the CQSW*. Study 3, London, CCETSW.

Szasz, T. (1962). *The Myth of Mental Illness*. London, Harper and Row.

Tiberius, R. (1986). Metaphors Underlying the Improvement of Teaching and Learning. *British Journal of Educational Technology*, 2(17), 144–56.

Towle, C. (1954). *The Learner in Education for the Professions as Seen in Education for Social Work*. Chicago, University of Chicago Press.

Van Rossum, E., Deijkers, R. and Hamer, R. (1985). Students' learning conceptions and their interpretation of significant learning concepts. *Higher Education* 14, 617–41.

Van Rossum, E. and Schenk, S. (1984). The relation between learning conception, study strategy and learning outcome. *British Journal of Educational Psychology*, 54, 73–83.

Wagner, R. and Sternberg, R. (1984). Alternative conceptions of intelligence and their implications for education. *Review of Educational Research*, 54, 179–224.

Watts, I. (1810). The improvement of the mind, in Entwistle and Hanley *op. cit.* (1977).

West, J. (1984). Student, supervisor, and personality type, *FSU Quarterly*, Family Service Units.

Whittington, C. (1986). Transfer of learning in social work education – a literature review. *British Journal of Social Work*, 571–77.

Whittington, C. and Holland R. (1985). A framework for theory in social work. *Issues in Social Work Education*, 5(1), 25–50.

Wilson, J. (1981). *Student Learning in Higher Education*. London, Croom Helm.

Witkin, H. Moore, C. *et al.* (1977). Role of the field-dependent and field-independent cognitive styles in academic evolution: a longitudinal study. *Journal of Educational Psychology*, 69(3), 197–211.

Wollman, W. (1984). Models and procedures: teaching for transfer of pendulum knowledge. *Research in Science Teaching*, 21(4), 399–415.

Young, P. (1967). *The Student and Supervision in Social Work*. London, Routledge and Kegan Paul.

Index

The Society for Research into Higher Education

The Society exists both to encourage and co-ordinate research and development into all aspects of Higher Education, including academic, organizational and policy issues; and also to provide a forum for debate – verbal and printed.

The Society's income derives from subscriptions, book sales, conference fees and grants. It receives no subsidies and is wholly independent. Its corporate members are institutions of higher education, research institutions and professional, industrial, and governmental bodies. Its individual members include teachers and researchers, administrators and students. Members are found in all parts of the world and the Society regards its international work as amongst its most important activities.

The Society discusses and comments on policy, organizes conferences and encourages research. Under the imprint SRHE & OPEN UNIVERSITY PRESS, it is a specialist publisher, having some 40 titles in print. It also publishes *Studies in Higher Education* (three times a year) which is mainly concerned with academic issues; *Higher Education Quarterly* (formerly *Universities Quarterly*) mainly concerned with policy issues; *Abstracts* (three times a year); an *International Newsletter* (twice a year) and *SRHE News* (four times a year).

The Society's committees, study groups and branches are run by members (with help from a small secretariat at Guildford), and aim to provide a forum for discussion. The groups at present include a Teacher Education Study Group, a Staff Development Group, a Women in Higher Education Group and a Continuing Education Group each of which may have their own organization, subscriptions or publications (e.g. the *Staff Development Newsletter*). A further Questions of Quality Group has organized a series of Anglo-American seminars in the USA and the UK.

The Governing Council, elected by members, comments on current issues; and discusses policies with leading figures, notably at its evening Forums. The Society organizes seminars on current research, and is in touch with bodies in the UK such as the NAB, CVCP, UGC, CNAA and with sister-bodies overseas. It cooperates with the British Council on courses run in conjunction with its conferences.

The Society's conferences are often held jointly and have considered 'Standards and Criteria in Higher Education' (1986, with Bulmershe College); 'Restructuring' (1987, with the City of Birmingham Polytechnic); 'Academic Freedom' (1988, the University of Surrey). In 1989, 'Access and Institutional Change' (with the Polytechnic of North London). In 1990 the topic will be 'Industry and Higher Education' (with the University of Surrey). In 1991 the topic will be 'Research in Higher Education'. Other conferences have considered the DES 'Green Paper' (1985) 'HE after the Election' (1987) and 'After the Reform Act' (1988). An annual series on 'The First-Year Experience' with the University of South Carolina and Teesside Polytechnic held two meetings in 1988 in

Cambridge, and another in St Andrew's in July 1989. For some of the Society's conferences, special studies are commissioned in advance, as 'Precedings'.

Members receive free of charge the Society's *Abstracts*, annual conference Proceedings (or 'Precedings'), *SHRE News and International Newsletter* and may buy SRHE & OPEN UNIVERSITY PRESS books at discount and *Higher Education Quarterly* on special terms. Corporate members also receive the Society's journal *Studies in Higher Education* free (individuals on special terms). Members may also obtain certain other journals at a discount, including the NFER *Register of Educational Research*. There is a substantial discount to members, and to staff of corporate members, on annual and some other conference fees.

Further information from SRHE at the University, Guildford, GU2 5XH.